A WISCONSIN TRAI:

GREAT
WISCONSIN
RESTAURANTS

101 FABULOUS CHOICES
BY THE MILWAUKEE JOURNAL SENTINEL'S
RESTAURANT CRITIC

DENNIS GETTO

WISCONSIN TRAILS
Madison, Wisconsin

First edition, first printing
Copyright © Dennis Getto

Library of Congress Catalog Card Number: 97-61673
ISBN: 0-915024-60-8

Editor: Elizabeth McBride
Designer: Kathie Campbell
Cover photograph: The White Gull Inn by Bill Paulson

Printed in the United States of America by Master Litho.

Wisconsin Tales and Trails
P.O. Box 5650
Madison, WI 53705
(800) 236-8088

To George J. Lockwood,
who made my career possible.

Contents

Southern Wisconsin

▼ ▼ ▼ ▼ ▼ ▼ ▼ ▼ ▼ ▼ ▼ ▼ ▼ ▼ ▼

Introduction

What makes a restaurant great?
That's a question I ask myself each week as restaurant critic for the *Milwaukee Journal Sentinel*.

For some diners, the most important element of a meal is atmosphere. Give them soft music and a sunset over a lake, and the meal is sure to be memorable. For others, service is the major concern. These diners look for a well-dressed host or hostess who greets them at the door and for a staff that paces the meal perfectly and serves with precision.

But while atmosphere and service are important components of a great restaurant meal, for me food counts the most. In general, I can overlook a long wait for my entree, and I can abide a hovering waiter or waitress, provided the meal I'm served offers some genuine excitement. That doesn't mean the meal has to follow the latest culinary fads. But it does have to be made well and from scratch. The flavor of commercial base in soup or the use of prepared frozen entrees, for example, are compromises that I'd rather not see.

That doesn't mean all the restaurants listed in this book hand-cut their French fries nightly or always top their desserts with real whipped cream. The restaurant business, like life, requires compromises. I don't always completely discount a restaurant for these practices, but as a restaurant critic, I routinely point out shortcomings like frozen vegetables or artificial dairy products.

With good food as my primary value, my first step in critiquing a restaurant is to see how it presents itself. If the restaurant is billed as a diner and delivers authentic, flavorful, made-from-scratch meals, I'll rate it highly. On the other hand, I will routinely dismiss inaccuracy whenever I see it. A Cajun restaurant, for example, that serves a stew and rice separately and calls it jambalaya is doing its customers a disservice—the real Louisianian dish combines all the ingredients early in the cooking process so the rice absorbs the wonderful flavors of the other ingredients. The same hold true for French, Italian and, to some extent, Chinese food. A restaurant that sautes a chicken breast, covers it with wine sauce and calls it coq au vin may be serving a good entree, but it's not coq au vin, which is a hearty French stew of chicken in red wine. A restaurant that bills itself as northern Italian ought to have polenta on the menu, along with some pastas in true cream sauces. These are the staples of northern Italian cuisine. And I tire of Chinese establishments that call an entree Sichuan beef and then serve soft pieces of meat in pepper gravy. True Sichuan beef is cut into matchstick-sized pieces and dry-cooked until it's chewy. The dish is prized for this consistency as much as for its flavor.

I rate culinary creativity highly. I especially favor chefs who take advantage of locally produced foods. Wisconsin is known for fine veal and duck, fresh

▼ ▼ ▼ ▼ ▼ ▼ ▼ ▼ ▼ ▼ ▼ ▼ ▼ ▼ ▼ ▼ ▼

whitefish, walleye and trout, wonderful cheeses and fresh fruits and vegetables. The most accomplished chefs showcase these excellent ingredients.

Some restaurant critics have minimum requirements for very good or excellent ratings. They demand tablecloths, fresh flowers on the tables and a separate coat room. Nothing in my evaluation system is so strict. Yet once I see white tablecloths, tuxedo-shirted servers and full five-piece place settings, my expectations rise. I expect the restaurant's food to be prepared with the same attention to detail.

Restaurant criticism must be done anonymously, and at all but a handful of restaurants I dine unannounced and am unrecognized by the staff. If I have questions about the food or the history of the establishment, I pose them by telephone after my visits are made. In this way, I enter a restaurant just as you do, expecting nothing more than to be treated like any other diner. I generally make two visits to each restaurant and will go back for a third or a fourth when I encounter a large menu and want to test the depth of the chef's expertise. In general, I order more elaborate entrees for the same reason. Properly grilling a steak is an art, but the skill it requires is minimal compared to the production of a more involved dish with complex flavors.

Although food is the most important factor in my ratings, I don't ignore service. One restaurant that I reviewed years ago had creative, interesting food, but plates arrived at the table as gracefully as incoming artillery shells. When I saw similar service gaffes during a subsequent visit, I lowered my appraisal of the establishment. The same standard holds for cleanliness. I once dined with a former inspector for a national chain. He led me to the men's room and ran his finger over the top of the room's privacy screens in a search for any build-up of dust that the cleaning crew might have ignored. I am not quite this strict, but I do expect a restaurant to be clean and its staff to handle silverware by the handles and stemware by its stems and to not put their fingers on the tines of the forks or the lips of the glasses.

Ambiance is harder to judge, but there is a universal standard: Restaurant patrons should feel as if they have just walked into the owner or manager's living room. It's hard to gauge an attitude, but I know it when I feel it. And it's my hope that you, too, will experience this kind of welcome at many of the restaurants that I've listed in this book.

Here are some things to consider as you make your dining selections:

Location. I have tried to suggest restaurants in all areas of the state. But in order to survive economically, restaurants must be close to prospective patrons. It follows that the largest number of restaurants listed here are in the highly populated southern third of the state.

Menu. Since the late 1970s, Wisconsin's restaurants have become more sophisticated. More and more chefs and owners are professionally trained, and some of the best have come from other countries. Many of this generation rewrite their menus seasonally, weekly or daily. So don't be disappointed if a dish that I have mentioned isn't on the menu the night you visit.

▼ ▼ ▼ ▼ ▼ ▼ ▼ ▼ ▼ ▼ ▼ ▼ ▼ ▼ ▼ ▼ ▼

Call ahead. Many restaurant owners, especially those in the North, close for vacation during the slower months (late-November to mid-April). Nothing's more disappointing than driving several hundred miles only to find your chosen restaurant closed. Calling ahead will also ensure a restaurant is still in business. One of the characteristics I looked for when selecting the restaurants for this book was stability. But the restaurant business is volatile and the majority of new restaurants that open fail in their first two years.

Handicapped access. Wisconsin law requires handicapped access in new buildings or those undergoing remodeling, but many older places have not updated their facilities. Others may have installed a ramp to the front door but have not replaced stairs leading to the restrooms. Sometimes older restrooms are too narrow for wheelchair access or lack handrails. Because of this variability, those with handicaps would be wise to call a restaurant before visiting to make sure their needs will be accommodated.

Smoking policy. Smoking in Wisconsin restaurants is problematic. Wisconsin law requires larger restaurants to provide seats for their nonsmoking patrons, but a lot of latitude is allowed. Sometimes the nonsmoking section is simply half or a corner of an open dining room, and smoke can still be a problem. In Madison, smoking in restaurants is prohibited, and many of the better restaurants in Milwaukee have banned smoking in their dining rooms. But others establishments, especially those that attract European or Asian clientele, still allow smoking. Included here is each restaurant's smoking policy at the time of publication. But if cigarette smoke ruins a meal for you, consider calling ahead to ask for the current smoking policy.

Hours. One of the biggest drawbacks to dining out in Wisconsin is that few good restaurants are open on Sunday. Wisconsin prides itself in being a family state, and most owners and chefs take Sunday off to be with their families. When you select a restaurant to visit on a Sunday, be sure you also note its hours of operation.

Vegetarian dishes. While new culinary trends have caught on, Wisconsin remains a meat-eating state. (One notable exception is Madison, where most restaurants offer at least one vegetarian entree and often feature several.) If you are vegetarian, your may find your best choices at Italian, Chinese and Middle Eastern establishments, which often have several meatless selections on the menu.

My goal in writing this book has been to list those restaurants that I have visited and consider to be great. I've made no attempt to rate them or to even say that the 101 places included here are the "best." New restaurants open constantly and, while my travels have been wide, I may have missed some restaurants that are worthy of note. Therefore, if you discover a restaurant that you think deserves mention, write to me in care of Wisconsin Trails (P.O. Box 5650, Madison, WI 53705). All suggestions will be considered for future editions.

I hope that this book will serve as a good working guide as you travel throughout Wisconsin. May it lead you to those wonderful little spots where a meal lives on in your memory for years to come.

Northern Wisconsin

▼ ▼ ▼ ▼ ▼ ▼ ▼ ▼ ▼ ▼ ▼ ▼ ▼ ▼ ▼ ▼ ▼

Arbor Vitae

The Plantation
Highways 51 and 70 East
(715) 356-9000

Any history of the Minocqua area has to include a mention of the Plantation. When the restaurant opened in 1938, it quickly became known for its elaborate floor shows, slot machines, crap tables, horse betting and excellent fried chicken. An armed robbery, during which a night watchman was killed, closed the club that same year. In 1939, the club reopened and began catering to a more respectable crowd. Even though the original building was destroyed by fire in 1974, the Plantation still offers some of the best fried chicken you'll find anywhere in the state.

The restaurant looks formal from the outside but has a contemporary interior, with ornate chandeliers and fresh flowers on the tables. Most diners dress casually. The menu is traditional American. Meals begin with complimentary appetizers called cheezies—small slices of rye bread topped with mayonnaise, onions and cheese and served hot from the oven. In addition to fried chicken, house specialties include a one-pound lobster tail, barbecued ribs and 14-ounce filet mignon steaks, which are served with wispy onion rings. Entrees come with salad and soup. Cream of asparagus and Dutch potato are the most popular soups.

Owners Tom and Lynn Gumhold take pride in their good food and an egalitarian approach to service. When Wisconsin's former governor Lee S. Dreyfus visited the Plantation on a busy Friday night in the early 1980s, the Gumholds made sure that he waited for a table just like everyone else.

Open 5 to 10 p.m. Tuesday through Sunday. Closed Monday. Dinner $$ to $$$. All major credit cards accepted. No smoking allowed.

Price Key

$	Under $10
$$	$10 to $15
$$$	$15 to $20
$$$$	$20 to $25
$$$$$	$25 to $30

Prices are for a single entree. Menus and hours of operation frequently change. Call ahead to avoid disappointment.

▼ ▼ ▼ ▼ ▼ ▼ ▼ ▼ ▼ ▼ ▼ ▼ ▼ ▼ ▼ ▼ ▼

The Old Rittenhouse Inn
301 Rittenhouse Avenue
(715) 779-5111

If you love Victorian mansions and wonderful food, make the journey to Bayfield, on Wisconsin's northernmost tip. There you'll find the Rittenhouse Inn, operated by Mary and Jerry Phillips, who, in the mid-1970s, opened the inn as one of the first bed and breakfast establishments in the state. In the two decades that have followed, the couple have distinguished themselves as chefs as well as innkeepers.

The building is a restored Queen Anne-style mansion built more than a hundred years ago. In the summer, containers of bright impatiens, fuschia and geraniums add little bursts of color to the building's red brick exterior.

Dinners at the Rittenhouse are fixed price, and there's no written menu. Instead, everything available from soups to desserts is announced—with an elaborate description—by the servers. The Phillips emphasize fresh ingredients, and the menu showcases local foods whenever possible. If you visit in early summer, you might have the opportunity to taste fresh cherry-champagne soup made from locally grown cherries. Whitefish and lake trout, often caught from nearby Lake Superior, are featured prominently in appetizers and entrees.

Dinner might start with fresh greens or a chilled lake trout salad that features hickory-smoked fish topped with cheddar cheese, fresh chives and fresh dill on a bed of wild rice with a creamy horseradish sauce. Salads are served with a basket of freshly made breads and rolls and some of the inn's homemade preserves. Soup might be the chilled cherry champagne or roast pumpkin pureed with fresh cream, sherry, nutmeg and a touch of curry powder.

During one visit to the Rittenhouse, a friend and I had leg of spring lamb that had been slow-roasted in red zinfandel wine with fresh homemade mint jelly and fresh whitefish and lake trout, layered with Swiss chard and cream. The fish were baked inside a fragile, flaky pastry crust. Choosing a dessert was difficult: Six were offered, including fresh crepes with homemade chocolate or rum sauce (or both); poached pears on a bed of stiff whipped cream; white chocolate torte with red raspberries; and English walnut cake, sliced into thin layers, brushed with chocolate liqueur, sprinkled with fresh raspberries, and then layered and frosted with white chocolate butter cream. The torte was the clear winner.

Open 5 to 9 p.m. nightly. (Reservations are recommended.) Dinner $$$$$. MasterCard and Visa accepted. No smoking allowed.

▼ ▼ ▼ ▼ ▼ ▼ ▼ ▼ ▼ ▼ ▼ ▼ ▼ ▼ ▼ ▼

Boulder Junction

The Guide's Inn

5421 Park Street (County M)
(715) 385-2233

What images flash through your mind when you think of a place called the Guide's Inn in Northern Wisconsin? Knotty pine walls. A long bar, with a lot of beer-swilling fishermen. Trophy fish mounted on every inch of the wall. And microwave pizzas.

Put all those images out of your mind as you drive to Boulder Junction for dinner at the Guide's Inn.

This North Woods restaurant is nicer than a lot of places farther south. There is a trophy musky in a showcase and a few other prize fish in the bar, along with paintings and pictures of the late famed guide, Porter Dean. But unlike many claustrophobic North Woods taverns, this restaurant's dining room has spacious windows that look out onto the woods, tasteful prints of colorful ducks, and soft cloth wallpaper with muted pine bough designs. That attractive, subdued decor, along with the inn's great food and service, make it a top spot by any standard.

The man behind the restaurant is chef and owner James Van Rossum, who keeps the restaurant open year-round to capitalize on the growing winter tourism. Two of his most popular dishes are pan-fried walleye and beef Wellington. The former is simply done; the latter is a bit more complicated. To make the Wellington, Van Rossum covers a tenderloin steak with mushrooms, scallions and a light liver spread, then wraps it in flaky pastry that's baked to a luscious light brown.

The restaurant also serves a famous Wisconsin snack: batter-fried cheese curds that are some of the best you'll find in Badgerland. Desserts are also good. Van Rossum makes refreshing sorbets and ice creams nightly and his apple strudel can match any made in Vienna.

Open 5 to 10 p.m. nightly. Dinner $$ to $$$$. MasterCard and Visa accepted. Smoking and nonsmoking sections available.

▼ ▼ ▼ ▼ ▼ ▼ ▼ ▼ ▼ ▼ ▼ ▼ ▼ ▼ ▼ ▼ ▼

Eau Claire

Fanny Hill
3919 Crescent Avenue
(715) 836-8184

I f you ask someone from Eau Claire to direct you to the best place in the area to have dinner, he or she may tell you to head for "The Hill." That's Fanny Hill, a combination restaurant, bed and breakfast, and theater located on a beautiful hillside a mile southwest of the Eau Claire city limits.

The decor is impressive from the moment you set foot inside. On the way to the dining room, you'll pass a small artificial waterfall and an ornate bar inhabited by a menagerie of teddy bears. The dining room's main attraction is its large picture windows, which are framed by Victorian woodwork and intricate lace valences. They provide a breathtaking view of the Chippewa River Valley and of the restaurant's grounds. In summer, hummingbirds dart among the flowers, and bright yellow goldfinches cling to feeders that are filled with thistle seed and hang just outside the windows. In the evening, brass candle lamps spread soft yellow light over each of the tables.

Fanny Hill's menu features a lot of New Orleans-style food, all of which is served by waiters and waitresses in tuxedo shirts and bow ties. Among the most popular items are tenderloin au poivre, which is rolled in crushed black peppercorns, sauteed and served with portabello mushrooms and caramelized apples, and catfish creole, which is pan-blackened with zucchini and red and green bell peppers. Black bean salsa finishes the dish. A wide range of desserts is available. On my last visit, pecan pie and Granny Smith apple-cranberry torte were both very good.

Open 5 to 9:30 p.m. Monday through Saturday; 10 a.m. to 9:30 p.m. Sunday. Lunch and dinner $ to $$$$. All major credit cards accepted. No smoking allowed.

▼ ▼ ▼ ▼ ▼ ▼ ▼ ▼ ▼ ▼ ▼ ▼ ▼ ▼ ▼ ▼ ▼

Egg Harbor

Trio
4655 County E
(920) 868-2090

Coming up with a name for their new restaurant wasn't particularly difficult for Jerry Spitz, Ron Perley and Mark Van Laanen. There were three of them, so they named the establishment Trio. Ideas for the restaurant's design came just as easily. The co-owners wanted to serve classic country dishes from Italy and France, so they built the restaurant to look like a farmhouse in southern France or central Italy. Instead of the typical white wood-frame construction found throughout Door County, Trio is made of brown stucco and has a Mediterranean feel.

Classic European peasant dishes frequently appear on the menu. One night you may have a chance to sample beef bourguignonne, a fragrant stew of beef in red wine; on another, cassoulet, a stew of white beans from southwestern France, might be offered. Or you might choose an Italian offering like linguine with meat-and-tomato Bolognese sauce or something a little trendier, such as bow-tie pasta with bacon and smoked salmon. Dessert is a must here: Tarts and other pastries usually feature the best fruits of the season.

All the food at Trio is apt to be delicious, and the restaurant's casual country atmosphere makes it all the more enjoyable. Wine is served in short tumblers, and pictures of pigs, roosters and vegetables decorate the walls.

Open 5 to 9:30 p.m. Sunday through Friday; 5 to 10 p.m. Saturday from the first weekend in May until the third weekend in October. Dinner $ to $$$. Master-Card, Visa, American Express and Discover accepted. No smoking allowed.

Price Key	
$	Under $10
$$	$10 to $15
$$$	$15 to $20
$$$$	$20 to $25
$$$$$	$25 to $30

Prices are for a single entree. Menus and hours of operation frequently change. Call ahead to avoid disappointment.

▼ ▼ ▼ ▼ ▼ ▼ ▼ ▼ ▼ ▼ ▼ ▼ ▼ ▼ ▼ ▼ ▼

Fish Creek
The Black Locust
4020 Highway 42
(920) 868-2999

You can't drive into the entrance of Peninsula State Park without seeing this wonderful restaurant and its attractive sign with a locust-tree logo. One of a new generation of exciting restaurants in Door County, the Black Locust showcases fresh seasonal foods, much of it locally produced, on an ever-changing menu.

The century-old building was the home and office of Bruce and Kathy Pepin, who owned the adjacent Peninsula Motel. Their daughter, Amy Kuhnz, and her husband, Christopher, converted the building to a restaurant in 1993. The couple did much of the work themselves. Among the surprises that they found were three layers of ceiling and earth-packed walls. The remodeling created a simple but elegant 15-table dining room with huge windows that let diners enjoy the magic of Door County's changing seasons.

And there's magic on the tables as well. All the dishes combine flavors in unusual and exciting ways. Christopher Kuhnz might sear a veal chop at a high temperature to produce a charred exterior that contrasts with the mild flavor of the inner meat. The chop is then set atop a carefully braised leek so that the diner enjoys oniony bites of yet another contrasting flavor. If it's early summer, Kuhnz will probably put some crunchy Door County asparagus on the side.

His au gratin potatoes are covered, as they are in France, with a mild white Swiss cheese sauce rather than the brash Colby that's more common in this country. Duck is artfully arranged around a mound of seared tender salad greens, prosciutto and pine nuts, and served with a sauce of dried Door County cherries. More pine nuts and almond slices link the mix to the taste of the wild rice pilaf beside it.

For dessert, there might be slices of stiff, rich chocolate mousse rolled in pistachios with a sauce of cherries, raspberries and huckleberries. Even better is Chef Kuhnz's wonderful Door County cherry crisp, crunchy with pecans and served warm with a scoop of vanilla ice cream dancing across its crust.

Open 5:30 to 10 p.m. nightly Memorial Day through October; 5:30 to 10 p.m. Thursday, Friday and Saturday the rest of the year. Dinner $$$ to $$$$$. MasterCard, Visa and Discover accepted. Smoking and nonsmoking sections available.

▼ ▼ ▼ ▼ ▼ ▼ ▼ ▼ ▼ ▼ ▼ ▼ ▼ ▼ ▼ ▼ ▼

EXTRA TIP
Door County Fish Boils

If you desire a traditional dinner in Door County, consider a fish boil. The practice of boiling Lake Michigan whitefish goes back to the early days of Door County, when Scandinavian fishermen cooked some of their catch in salted water with new potatoes and arranged both on a plate with bread to make a meal.

Along with good food, fish boils, widely held in summer, provide something of a spectacle. The cooking process begins with a hot hardwood fire over which a kettle of salted water is brought to a boil. Then the fish, potatoes and, at some locations, onions are added and cooked for several minutes. When these ingredients are done, the cook throws a small quantity of kerosene onto the flames. The resulting fireball makes the pot boil over. This last step clears the kettle of the fishy-tasting oils that have floated to the top of the water during cooking. The boiled fish and potatoes are then served with fresh coleslaw and an assortment of breads. Door County tradition mandates that the meal be finished off with a slice of cherry pie.

The restaurants that offer fish boils usually advertise them on signs outside. Simply drive up Highway 42 or Highway 57 and stop at the spot that most interests you.

▼ ▼ ▼ ▼ ▼ ▼ ▼ ▼ ▼ ▼ ▼ ▼ ▼ ▼ ▼ ▼

The Cookery
4135 Main Street (Highway 42)
(920) 868-3634

The story of this casual, moderately priced restaurant on Fish Creek's main drag begins with a honeymoon. In 1977, Dick and Carol Skare of Minneapolis were spending the first few days of their married life in Door County and liked the quiet atmosphere they found there. They moved to the area and bought a 20-seat restaurant called the Blue Willow. Both the Skares wanted to give Door County residents a healthy alternative to Wisconsin's heavier foods. They also wanted to showcase locally produced foods, such as whitefish and cherries.

The concept caught on quickly. In 1980, the Skares had to expand the restaurant's seating to 85. In 1984, they added the Pantry, a separate operation that sells jams and cherry chutney, along with an extensive line of breads, muffins and other baked goods. Today, it's common to wait for a seat at the restaurant on weekends. And the menu includes a selection of low-fat, low-calorie entrees. A wonderful whitefish chowder is available, along with several healthy chicken breast entrees. There's also fresh lake perch, a Wisconsin delicacy.

Whatever you do, leave room for a slice of cherry pie or a piece of the Cookery's cherry crisp. And pick up a jar of cherry chutney on your way out. At home, you can make a great appetizer by spreading the chutney over a layer of cream cheese and scraping up both with crackers.

Open 7 a.m. to 9 p.m. daily from Memorial Day through October; 7 a.m. to 8 p.m. Friday and Saturday, 7 a.m. to 3 p.m. Sunday in November. Closed December, except for Christmas week. Open 7:30 a.m. to 8 p.m. Friday and Saturday, 7:30 a.m. to 3 p.m. Sunday from New Year's Day until the second weekend in April; 7 a.m. to 8 p.m. daily from the third weekend in April to Memorial Day. Breakfast, lunch and dinner $ to $$. MasterCard and Visa accepted. No smoking allowed.

▼ ▼ ▼ ▼ ▼ ▼ ▼ ▼ ▼ ▼ ▼ ▼ ▼ ▼ ▼ ▼ ▼ ▼

Fish Creek

The White Gull Inn

4225 Main Street
(920) 868-3517

The White Gull Inn is one of the most historic spots in Door County. It was established at the turn of the century as a summer resort by a doctor who had several of the buildings moved onto the site from Marinette. The buildings were towed across the frozen waters of Green Bay during the winter months. In 1972, Andy and Jan Coulson bought the inn. Today, in addition to providing lodging, the White Gull is one of the premier spots for a fish boil, which can be especially impressive on a late fall evening when sparks from the wood fire dance with the first snowflakes of winter.

The fish boil includes potatoes, coleslaw, homemade breads and cherry pie, along with the fish. More elaborate candlelight dinners are served on the nights when the fish boil is not offered. Fresh whitefish appears on the menu, when available, along with beef Wellington and fresh scallops in orange liqueur sauce. Raspberry chicken amandine, shrimp artichoke Romano and stuffed steaks are other frequently served dishes.

Breakfast and lunch are also great meals to have here. Two of the most popular breakfast dishes are French toast, stuffed with cream cheese and Door County cherries, and cherry pancakes. At lunch, the inn is known for its fresh whitefish sandwiches and grilled chicken breast salad, topped with toasted pecans and honey-lime dressing.

If you're planning to attend the fish boil, be sure to call for a reservation. Seats fill up fast during the tourist season.

Open 7:30 a.m. to 2:30 p.m. daily. Fish boils served at 5:45, 7 and 8:15 p.m. Wednesday, Friday, Saturday and Sunday Memorial Day through October; Wednesday and Saturday the rest of the year. On non-fish-boil nights, dinner is served 5 to 8 p.m. Breakfast, lunch and dinner $ to $$$. All major credit cards accepted. No smoking allowed.

▼ ▼ ▼ ▼ ▼ ▼ ▼ ▼ ▼ ▼ ▼ ▼ ▼ ▼ ▼ ▼ ▼

Hayward
The Beach Club
County K
(715) 634-3090

Walk into the Beach Club on Lac Court Oreilles and, for a minute, you may wonder if you're still in the North Woods. Motorized surf boards hang on the walls. Tropical fans ply the air above you. And the host, dressed in shorts and a Hawaiian shirt, may greet you with an "Aloha!" The illusion will disappear as soon as you're seated in the Beach Club's dining room and look out onto the lake and the native Wisconsin pines that surround it.

Terry and Pam Fairclough, who opened the restaurant in 1995, have introduced an extensive menu that deviates pleasantly from traditional North Woods fare. The list of hot and cold appetizers includes alligator Creole, Jamaican shrimp and duck strudel, and the salad line-up features one salad that combines strawberries and spinach and another that has all the ingredients that go into a good bacon, lettuce and tomato sandwich.

Best of all is the list of entrees, which range from charbroiled chicken and steaks to lamb tenderloin with a Scotch whiskey sauce and walleye roasted in a crunchy nut crust. Desserts, such as strawberry shortcake, often feature the fruits of the season.

In the summer, there's seating outside on the deck. If you can, try to have dinner around sunset, when the lake view is especially beautiful.

Open 5 to 9 p.m. Tuesday through Thursday; 5 to 10 p.m. Friday and Saturday. Closed Sunday and Monday. Dinner $$ to $$$$$. All major credit cards accepted. Smoking and nonsmoking sections available.

Price Key
$	Under $10
$$	$10 to $15
$$$	$15 to $20
$$$$	$20 to $25
$$$$$	$25 to $30

Prices are for a single entree. Menus and hours of operation frequently change. Call ahead to avoid disappointment.

11

▼ ▼ ▼ ▼ ▼ ▼ ▼ ▼ ▼ ▼ ▼ ▼ ▼ ▼ ▼ ▼

Hayward

Famous Dave's BBQ Shack
County B and Moreland Road
(715) 462-3352

Names can be deceiving. Famous Dave's, 8½ miles east of Hayward, does serve barbecued ribs, brisket and chicken good enough to deserve fame. But the restaurant is no shack.

Built of huge pine logs, with a huge stone fireplace dominating both of its dining rooms, the sprawling 325-seat restaurant is lavish by North Woods standards. Large windows on the west side of the building look out onto Big Round Lake, television monitors sit in every corner of the bar, and rotisserie ovens filled with slow-roasting chickens line one wall. The decor is an odd collection of antique straw hats, old beer signs, books, jars, ceramic pigs and a host of other collectibles stacked on shelves or hanging from the walls. Light is provided by deer-antler chandeliers, and the chairs in the bar still have their bark on them.

The restaurant is named for its owner, Dave Anderson, who helped to develop the Rainforest Café chain of restaurants and is on that company's board of directors. As a boy growing up on the West Side of Chicago, Dave vacationed in Hayward with his family and liked the area so much that he bought an old resort, razed it and built the BBQ Shack and adjacent Grand Pines Resort.

The restaurant's main attraction is barbecued ribs slathered with a slightly sweet sauce that Anderson himself developed. Barbecued chicken and beef brisket are also excellent, as is the restaurant's Southern-fried chicken. A full dinner at Famous Dave's includes additional delicacies: Wilbur beans, which are flavored with thin slices of smoked sausage; corn on the cob; a cornbread muffin; and a choice of horseradish-enhanced cole slaw or creamy potato salad. Famous Dave's also offers "Up North" specials, such as wild rice soup and walleye. As for desserts, Famous Dave's bread pudding alone is enough to make Dave famous.

On weekends, the restaurant serves an expansive breakfast buffet with Smokehouse hash, eggs Benedict, fresh fruit, cinnamon rolls and made-to-order omelets.

Open 10:30 a.m. to 10 p.m. Monday, Tuesday and Wednesday; 8 a.m. to 10 p.m. Thursday and Sunday; 8 a.m. to 11 p.m. Friday and Saturday during the summer months. Call for winter hours. Breakfast, lunch and dinner $ to $$$$. All major credit cards accepted. No smoking allowed.

▼ ▼ ▼ ▼ ▼ ▼ ▼ ▼ ▼ ▼ ▼ ▼ ▼ ▼ ▼ ▼ ▼

Hazelhurst

Jacobi's of Hazelhurst

9820 Cedar Falls Road
(715) 356-5591

Some restaurants leave impressions that stay with you all your life. One of my fondest memories is of a dinner with friends at Jacobi's of Hazelhurst. It was early November, and we were seated at a table near a window that looked out onto the woods. A fire roared in the restaurant's fireplace. It was already dark, but enough light spilled from the building to see the big trees that stood beyond the restaurant's back yard. First one, then another of the season's first big snowflakes began drifting through the night air. They sparkled and danced as they parachuted to the ground. While I could have seen those first snowflakes from any window, it was owners Pam and Al Jacobi who provided me with such a wonderful setting for a meal.

Dinners start out with chef Al Jacobi's special complimentary appetizers, which give him a chance to satisfy his culinary fancy. One recent offering was Caribbean jerk chicken with chili bow ties and a Jamaica fire stick, which blends three cheeses and cayenne pepper. On other nights, he might serve Swedish meatballs with homemade pistachio bread.

Then it's on to entrees: Two of the restaurant's specialties are steaks—a garlic-stuffed beef tenderloin with cognac mustard sauce and steak au poivre in a brandy cream sauce. Another house specialty offers pork or veal sauteed with mushrooms and covered with Wisconsin bleu cheese.

The restaurant's a little difficult to find: To get there, drive five miles south from "downtown" Minocqua on Highway 51, then head west on Cedar Falls Road. After a quarter mile, look for the building that's painted Victorian pink and purple. If it's summer, be sure to notice Al Jacobi's flower garden.

Open 5 to 10 p.m. Tuesday through Sunday from the end of June to the third week of October; 5 to 9 p.m. Thursday and Friday, and 5 to 10 p.m. Saturday during the winter; 5 to10 p.m. Wednesday through Sunday during May and June. Dinner $$ to $$$$$. MasterCard and Visa accepted. No smoking allowed.

EXTRA TIP
Best Barbecues

While Wisconsin may not be as strong as the Southern states in the barbecue department, it does have some good spots for ribs and pulled pork sandwiches. Two of the best, **Piggy's of La Crosse** and **Jerry's Old Town**, are listed elsewhere in this book. For real barbecue fans, here are some other places around the state where you can indulge your passion:

Big Mama & Uncle Fats', 6824 Odana Road, Madison; (608) 829-2683. Ribs are served three ways at this casual 88-seat restaurant on Madison's West Side: Southern-style, with a vinegar-based sauce; Northern-style, with a tomato-based sauce; and "naked," which means covered with a dry rub of spices and served without sauce. The restaurant also offers an extensive menu of Southern delights. If you're looking for an interesting appetizer, try the deep-fried pickles. They may sound awful, but they taste great.

Mike's Smoke House, 2235 N. Clairemont Ave., Eau Claire; (715) 834-8153. As soon as you pull into the parking lot of this casual restaurant on the southwest side of Eau Claire, you'll notice the pungent aroma of burning hardwood. Inside, ribs, pork and other meats are slowly being barbecued. This is a great place for a pulled pork sandwich (the meat is pulled from the bone), served on a big chewy roll with great coleslaw on the side.

Brew City BBQ, 1114 N. Water St., Milwaukee; (414) 278-7033. This restaurant is especially fun in summer, when tables and chairs are set up outside. The ribs, prepared in a special smoker, are very good, as is barbecued chicken. After you've eaten, you can wash up in an industrial-style sink in the dining room.

▼ ▼ ▼ ▼ ▼ ▼ ▼ ▼ ▼ ▼ ▼ ▼ ▼ ▼ ▼ ▼ ▼

Madeline Island

The Clubhouse on Madeline Island
Old Fort Road
(715) 747-2612

Having dinner at this excellent restaurant on the largest of the Apostle Islands is one of the most charming experiences you can have in Wisconsin. You board the ferry in nearby Bayfield, and as you ride across to the island, the gentle rolling of Lake Superior rocks away your stress. The restaurant's van is waiting when the ferry docks. Its driver has your name and opens the door for you.

A short ride takes you to the 12-sided building that houses the Clubhouse restaurant. It was built in 1968 as part of a private club that included a near-by golf course. The club eventually dissolved. Mary Rice, a watercolor artist, bought the place in 1982. Her works hang in the restaurant.

Those watercolors are only part of the artwork featured at the Clubhouse. When it comes to creative appetizers and entrees, this restaurant is hard to beat. Dinners begin with small complimentary first courses, like wild rice soup with bleu cheese and apple, or delicate cheese puffs filled with smoked black beans and served with a dollop of chive-studded sour cream. Other "starters" on the menu might be a phyllo-dough Napoleon filled with home-smoked duck and *fourme d'Ambert* (a fetalike cheese). Then it's on to entrees like almond-crusted lake trout with mustard cream, and grilled veal loin with a ragout of roasted shiitake mushrooms, hazelnuts and shallots. Desserts include a perfectly made coffee-flavored creme brulee with a crunchy caramelized top, and a tasting plate that lets you sample fresh homemade vanilla ice cream, honey-nectarine sorbet and white chocolate mousse.

You'll enjoy another ferry ride back to the mainland. And as you watch the lights of Bayfield approach, you'll remember a wonderful meal.

Open 6 to 10 p.m. Wednesday through Sunday in July and August; 6 to 10 p.m. Thursday through Sunday in September. Closed the rest of the year. Dinner $$$$ to $$$$$. MasterCard, Visa, American Express and Discover accepted. No smoking allowed.

▼ ▼ ▼ ▼ ▼ ▼ ▼ ▼ ▼ ▼ ▼ ▼ ▼ ▼ ▼

Menomonie

The Bolo Country Inn
207 Pine Avenue
(800) 553-2656

There are lots of stories about dogs being dedicated to their masters. The story behind the Bolo Country Inn, however, is about a master who was dedicated to his dog. The master was the late Bill Braker, a local restaurateur who built the inn in 1968. The dog was Bolo, a black Labrador retriever that took second place in national field trials in 1948.

The inn is something of a monument to Braker's dog. Bolo's trophies are exhibited, and several portraits of him hang on the wall. Bolo's likeness appears on the restaurant's place mats and napkins, and his silhouette is cut into the lampshades in the bar. The bar's walls, of course, are covered with houndstooth wallpaper.

But you don't have to be a dog lover to love the Bolo Inn. The restaurant is run by Braker's children and benefits from its proximity to the University of Wisconsin—Stout, which has the state's premier restaurant management program. The inn's standards are high.

Like many restaurants in northwestern Wisconsin, steaks are a major attraction. One of the best is a special tenderloin heaped with sauteed mushrooms and served with a well-made brown sauce. Barbecued ribs and center-cut pork chops are house specialties, and main course salads, like the classic Cobb and the Bolo's own Hodge Podge, are very good. Dinners come with fresh popovers. The inn's strawberry shortcake has a light caramel sauce between the cake and its topping of berries and whipped cream.

Open 11 a.m. to 11 p.m. Friday and Saturday; 11 a.m. to 10 p.m. Sunday through Thursday. Lunch $ to $$; dinner $ to $$$$. MasterCard, Visa, American Express and Diner's Club accepted. Smoking and nonsmoking sections available.

▼ ▼ ▼ ▼ ▼ ▼ ▼ ▼ ▼ ▼ ▼ ▼ ▼ ▼ ▼ ▼ ▼

Sister Bay

Al Johnson's Swedish Restaurant and Butik
702 Bay Shore Drive (Highway 42)
(920) 854-2626

This landmark restaurant in Sister Bay has one characteristic that everyone remembers: a traditional Norwegian sod roof with goats to keep it trimmed. Many Wisconsinites simply refer to Al Johnson's as "the place with the goats on the roof."

But there's more here than just goats and second-story sod. The building was first assembled in Norway of Norwegian pine logs under the direction of architect George Mangan, a specialist in folk architecture. Then all the logs were numbered, and the building disassembled and shipped to Sister Bay, where four carpenters from Norway reassembled it.

The building houses a restaurant that's enormously popular, especially for breakfast. The main attraction is Swedish pancakes—delicate crepelike creations that taste best with an order of lingonberries on the side (one order of the berries is usually enough for two to three people). The pancakes are so good that many fans order them for lunch or dinner. Swedish meatballs are also popular, and if you're really hungry, you can get both on a combination platter. The menu offers standard American entrees and sandwiches, as well.

Expect to wait for a table, but waiting at Al Johnson's isn't necessarily a bad thing: The adjacent boutique specializes in clothing and other items from Scandinavia. They even stock real Swedish fish candy.

Open 6 a.m. to 9 p.m. daily in summer; 7 a.m. to 8 p.m. daily in winter. Breakfast, lunch and dinner $ to $$$. All major credit cards accepted. No smoking allowed.

Price Key
$	Under $10
$$	$10 to $15
$$$	$15 to $20
$$$$	$20 to $25
$$$$$	$25 to $30

Prices are for a single entree. Menus and hours of operation frequently change. Call ahead to avoid disappointment.

17

Sister Bay

Inn at Kristofer's
734 Bay Shore Drive (Highway 42)
(920) 854-9419

Hang around in the parking lot of this popular Door County restaurant and you just might see chef and co-owner Terri Milligan dash out the back door with a pair of scissors in hand. She'll head straight for the restaurant's well-tended herb garden, snip a few things and then dash back into the kitchen. She believes that fresh tastes best.

Over the past two years, the Inn at Kristofer's, which Milligan owns with her husband, Christopher, has become one of Door County's major culinary hubs. In addition to a wonderful restaurant downstairs, the couple have added a cooking school and commercial kitchen for catering upstairs. At night, the cooking school doubles as a waiting room for folks dining downstairs.

One of the restaurant's major assets is the beautiful view of Green Bay that it affords its diners. The others are the interesting entrees and the charming atmosphere that the Milligans have created. During the summer months, there's live music playing every night while dinners are served at a charming collection of antique tables. Several of the serving pieces are Depression glass.

Milligan's culinary offerings change nightly but always showcase local produce. In spring, there's likely to be locally grown asparagus with Milligan's own vinaigrette and bits of smoked salmon. The ever-changing list of entrees may include rack of lamb in a mustard crust or quail with Door County cherry sauce.

With only 12 tables and 46 seats inside (there are 12 more tables outside), the restaurant is one of the smallest in Door County. But its excellent food makes waiting for a table worthwhile.

Open 5 to 10 p.m. nightly May 1 to Nov. 1; 5 to 9 p.m. Thursday through Sunday from Nov. 1 to April 30. Dinner $ to $$$$. MasterCard and Visa accepted. No smoking allowed.

▼ ▼ ▼ ▼ ▼ ▼ ▼ ▼ ▼ ▼ ▼ ▼ ▼ ▼ ▼ ▼

The Whitetail Inn
9038 County C
(715) 542-2541

I n Northern Wisconsin, restaurants housed in old log cabins aren't that unusual. The Whitetail Inn is a notable exception. While most of northern Wisconsin's log cabins date to the late 19th or early 20th century, the Whitetail Inn was built in 1992. Most log cabins are small; the Whitetail Inn is massive. And its North Woods decor shows an atypical environmental sensitivity. The pine logs that make up the walls came from trees that were at the end of their life cycle, rather than trees harvested in their prime. The staghorn chandeliers were made by a firm in Montana that uses only naturally shed antlers. And the trophy deer heads that decorate the bar and dining rooms aren't real but masterful reproductions.

The Whitetail Inn serves good food. Hearty soups, such as beef with rice and shrimp Creole, are a house specialty. At lunch, there's a long sandwich line-up. At dinner, the inn offers great fish entrees, such as stuffed trout, grilled salmon and baked whitefish, when it's available. The inn's roast duck, prime rib and walleye pike are also good. Dinners are served with small loaves of warm fresh-baked bread. A children's menu is available.

Open 11 a.m. to 10 p.m. Monday through Saturday; 10 a.m. to 9 p.m. Sunday in the summer. Closed Mondays in winter. Lunch $; dinner $$ to $$$. MasterCard and Visa accepted. No smoking allowed.

▼ ▼ ▼ ▼ ▼ ▼ ▼ ▼ ▼ ▼ ▼ ▼ ▼ ▼ ▼ ▼ ▼

Sturgeon Bay

The Inn at Cedar Crossing

336 Louisiana Street
(920) 743-4249

If you're looking for Victorian charm or enjoy regional cuisine, plan to have a meal at this Sturgeon Bay inn. The 1884 building, located in the middle of historic downtown Sturgeon Bay, originally housed a drug store on the main floor, with living quarters above. In the century that followed, the downstairs space was occupied by a tailor shop, a soda fountain, a shoe store and a dentist's office. In 1986, Terry Wulf refurbished the building and reopened it as a historic country inn with nine rooms. In 1989, she opened the downstairs restaurant that specializes in fresh, made-from-scratch regional foods.

It's an elegant place, with walls trimmed in natural oak and stenciled with delicate wreath patterns. A flashy grapevine arrangement hangs over the marble and oak fireplace, and fresh flowers add color to the tables.

While the inn's look is Victorian, its menu is wonderfully contemporary, featuring fish, pasta, duckling, veal, lamb and pheasant. Dishes are decorated in a stunning fashion, with bouquets of flowers and berries, sometimes set in perfectly piped mounds of chived mashed potato. Breads and desserts are all homemade and not to be missed.

For a real treat, stop at the inn for Sunday brunch. You may find it hard to decide whether you want one of the delightfully fluffy omelets or thick French toast made with homemade bread.

Open 7 a.m. to 9 p.m. Sunday through Thursday; 7 a.m. to 9:30 p.m. Friday and Saturday. Breakfast, lunch and dinner $ to $$$. MasterCard, Visa and Discover accepted. No smoking allowed.

▼ ▼ ▼ ▼ ▼ ▼ ▼ ▼ ▼ ▼ ▼ ▼ ▼ ▼ ▼ ▼ ▼

Sugar Camp

The White Stag Inn
7141 Highway 17 North
(715) 272-1057

There are a couple of ways to establish a really good restaurant. One is to research exotic cuisines, master them and then delight your guests with unusual dishes. Another is to concentrate on a few familiar dishes and really do them right.

That second approach is the one that the Widule family has been taking at the White Stag Inn since Louis Widule started serving food there in 1957. The restaurant is now operated by sons David and Louis Widule and other family members.

The White Stag Inn is modeled after the steak houses that were in vogue in Chicago in the 1950s and remain popular today. Steaks, many of which are hand-cut in the restaurant's kitchen, play prominently on the menu. Pork chops, chicken, shrimp, fish and, most recently, farm-raised catfish, round out the offerings. All of those meats are cooked over a huge built-in fireplace that burns solid lump hardwood charcoal that the restaurant ships in from Virginia. The Widules prefer it to commercial briquets, which, they say, can impart an oily taste to food.

Side orders of mushrooms are skewered and grilled over the coals and taste especially good on the steaks. Baked potatoes are big and topped with a home-made mix of cottage cheese and chives. Salads are wedges of iceberg lettuce served in huge stainless-steel bowls with a selection of homemade dressings and a basket of fresh rolls. Desserts, like dinners, are simple but good—ice cream and sundaes.

The restaurant is hard to miss once you're on Highway 17. Just look for the large statue of the white stag outside.

Open 5 to 11 p.m. nightly from Memorial Day through October; 5 to 10 p.m. Sunday through Friday and 5 to 11 p.m. Saturday from November through May. Dinner $ to $$$$$. MasterCard, Visa and Diner's Club accepted. Smoking and nonsmoking sections available.

▼ ▼ ▼ ▼ ▼ ▼ ▼ ▼ ▼ ▼ ▼ ▼ ▼ ▼ ▼ ▼ ▼

Superior

The Library

1410 Tower Avenue
(715) 392-4821

Walk into this restaurant and you'll understand immediately how it got its name. The dining room is lined with shelves that hold hundreds of books. But though it may look like a library, the restaurant never was one.

Opened by Ted Cohen in 1977, the Library has become one of the area's most popular places for good food. Topping the list of entrees is steak, which is specially aged to yield tender, flavorful cuts. (The T-bone is especially good.) Ribs, covered with a respectable tomato-based sauce, are also popular, as are pasta dishes like chicken tetrazzini. And in the summer months, one of Lake Superior's finest delicacies—fresh whitefish—is broiled and served nightly.

While entrees are interesting and well-prepared, the Library's huge salad bar is also a major attraction. It features two homemade soups, hot sourdough bread, a great assortment of salad ingredients (including fresh fruit) and an extensive line-up of prepared salads, relishes and dressing.

Dinners at the Library also come with freshly made chicken liver spread and wonderful popovers, which are served with honey butter. If you have any room for dessert, the Library's cheesecake is the dessert of choice. And if you're interested in something more casual, the Zona Rosa Café, also owned by Cohen, is housed under the same roof.

Open 11 a.m. to 10 p.m. Monday through Saturday; 10 a.m. to 9 p.m. Sunday in the summer. Open 11 a.m. to 9 p.m. Monday through Thursday; 11 a.m. to 10 p.m. Friday and Saturday; and 10 a.m. to 8 p.m. Sunday in the winter. Lunch $ to $$; dinner $ to $$$$$. All major credit cards accepted.

▼ ▼ ▼ ▼ ▼ ▼ ▼ ▼ ▼ ▼ ▼ ▼ ▼ ▼ ▼ ▼ ▼

Superior
The Shack
3301 Belknap Street
(715) 392-9836

One of Superior-Duluth's most popular supper clubs began as a busy liquor store and bar owned by Paul and Gloria Heytens. When their business prospered, they decided to expand and add a restaurant. So in 1980, the couple built The Shack.

Don't be deceived by the name; this place is no shack. The restaurant is a pleasant spot for a meal, decorated in a garden motif, with trellis-work partitions and bright floral prints. The restaurant specializes in a formal Caesar salad that's prepared tableside, just as it is in many fancy restaurants.

These days, the Heytens' son, Patrick Heytens, and his wife, Rene, run the Shack, which has established a reputation for prime rib and crunchy-crusted fried chicken, served with warm whole-wheat bread. The restaurant also makes hearty homemade soups, like chicken dumpling, with lots of chicken, carrots, celery and—of course—homemade dumplings. In recent years, Pat Heytens has installed a hickory smoker that turns out smoked ribs, beef and pork, which are popular with the restaurant's regulars.

Open 4:30 to 9 p.m. Monday through Thursday; 4:30 to 10 p.m. Friday and Saturday; 11:30 a.m. to 8 p.m. Sunday. Lunch $; dinner $ to $$$. All major credit cards (except American Express) accepted. Smoking and nonsmoking sections available.

Wausau

The Peking
221 Scott Street
(715) 842-8080

Since its opening in 1980, this Chinese restaurant has drawn diners for two reasons. The first is its menu, which lists a variety of Chinese dishes, including spicy Sichuan delights. The second is the decor, which is reminiscent of the Roaring Twenties.

The Peking is located in what was once the ballroom of the old Landmark Hotel in downtown Wausau. The walls are adorned with ornate plaster, all painted in subtle pink tones. The long vintage bar is built of dark wood and would be at home in an F. Scott Fitzgerald novel.

To get the most from the menu, start with one of chef Jeff Cheng's soups, like his hot and sour soup, a sweet and spicy broth with Chinese mushrooms, carrots and tofu. From there, move on to a special, like Pork Shanghai, a noodle dish that combines shrimp, pork and cabbage in a slightly sweet chili sauce. Or try Ma Po bean curd, which Cheng makes with scallions, pork shreds, Chinese mushrooms, Chinese preserved vegetables and chunks of tofu. Or try another house favorite—Governor's chicken, with onions, peas, peanuts and hot chili peppers. If you want a Japanese accent, tempura chicken and vegetables are offered as side dishes.

Cheng also operates a second, smaller Peking at 1017 First Ave. in Woodruff. Even though it does not have the fancy atmosphere of the Wausau restaurant, the recipes are the same.

Open 11 a.m. to 2 p.m. and 4 to 9 p.m. Monday through Saturday. Closed Sunday, except on Mother's Day. Lunch and dinner $ to $$$. MasterCard, Visa and American Express accepted. Smoking and nonsmoking sections available.

Price Key
$	Under $10
$$	$10 to $15
$$$	$15 to $20
$$$$	$20 to $25
$$$$$	$25 to $30

Prices are for a single entree. Menus and hours of operation frequently change. Call ahead to avoid disappointment.

▼ ▼ ▼ ▼ ▼ ▼ ▼ ▼ ▼ ▼ ▼ ▼ ▼ ▼ ▼ ▼ ▼ ▼ ▼

EXTRA TIP
Food With a View

One of the best attributes you can find in a restaurant is a nice view. In Door County, for example, have dinner at the **Inn at Kristofer's**, and you'll also be treated to a good look at Green Bay, which is beautiful at sunset.

Several other restaurants listed in this book offer great views: **Eve's Supper Club** in Green Bay looks out over the Fox River and the Green Bay area, **Lake Park Bistro** in Milwaukee and the **Hobnob** in Kenosha offer views of Lake Michigan, **Fanny Hill** in Eau Claire provides a remarkable vista of the Chippewa River Valley, **Heidel House** has a commanding view of Green Lake, and **Famous Dave's BBQ Shack** looks out over Big Round Lake.

Two other restaurants are worthy of note:

The **Polaris**, atop the Hyatt Regency Hotel in Milwaukee (333 W. Kilbourn Ave.; 414-276-1234) is a revolving restaurant, 18 stories above street level. The restaurant makes a full rotation every 90 minutes and gives you a wonderful panorama of the city and Lake Michigan.

The **FireHouse on the River** in Prairie du Sac (540 Water St.; 608-643-2484) offers a lovely view of the Wisconsin River and the wooded bluffs that flank it. In February, the restaurant is exceptionally popular with bird watchers from around the state who come to see bald eagles feed in the open stretches of the river.

25

Central Wisconsin

▼ ▼ ▼ ▼ ▼ ▼ ▼ ▼ ▼ ▼ ▼ ▼ ▼ ▼ ▼ ▼ ▼

Allouez

Eve's Supper Club
2020 Riverside Drive
(920) 435-1571

The old saying about real estate holds that three things are important: location, location and location. The same is at least partially true for restaurants. One good example is Eve's Supper Club in the Green Bay suburb of Allouez.

Eve's occupies the top floor of a four-story office building and has huge picture windows that look out over the Fox River and the valley through which it runs. The view forms a delightful backdrop for lunch. It becomes even more attractive after dark, when the lights of the valley and the reflections of the river weave themselves into a sparkling tapestry. The panorama makes the supper club a romantic place. If you're looking for the right spot for a quiet meal with someone special, wait for a window-side table.

Unlike real estate, however, restaurants also need to provide good service and food, and Eve's delivers both. The restaurant's staff goes out of its way to make guests feel welcome. At one dinner visit several years ago, a youngster in our party spilled a glass of soda. We were mopping it up when our server considerately moved us to a different table.

That welcome feeling may be due to the fact that Eve's has been a family business for 30 years. The restaurant is named after Eve Haltaufderheid, who works as the supper club's hostess; one son, Rick Haltaufderheid, is the restaurant's executive chef; another son, Jerry Haltaufderheid is a bartender; and daughter-in-law Jarreth works as a waitress.

The most popular item on Eve's menu is steak, and several cuts are offered, along with prime rib and lamb chops. The restaurant also specializes in fresh whitefish, trout and salmon. Several combination dishes let diners try both fish and meat. Dinners start with a relish tray that features homemade cheese spreads and soups that are hearty and well-made.

Open 11 a.m. to 2 p.m. Monday through Friday; 5 to 10 p.m. Monday through Saturday. Closed Sunday. Lunch $; dinner $$ to $$$. All major credit cards accepted. Smoking and nonsmoking sections available.

▼ ▼ ▼ ▼ ▼ ▼ ▼ ▼ ▼ ▼ ▼ ▼ ▼ ▼ ▼ ▼

Appleton

Peggy's

125 East College Avenue
(920) 830-1971

You've probably heard, hundreds of times, that too many cooks spoil the broth. But did you ever wonder how many cooks are too many? At Peggy's five chefs work in the kitchen. And while all five don't work the same hours, Peggy's team of professionals is something of a culinary brain trust. Members work together to develop new dishes that combine various ingredients and flavors.

Many of those creations make their way onto Peggy's menu, which changes daily. One appetizer that appears frequently, jacket and Thai chicken, blends Oriental and Mexican flavors. The dish starts with tender chunks of chicken breast marinated in cilantro and lime. The chicken is grilled and wrapped in hot wheat tortillas and served with fresh mango salsa and cilantro lime sour cream on the side.

Dinner can provide a tour of the world. You might start with a crispy appetizer pizza or a French country platter with thick slabs of country pate and vegetable terrine. You might follow with an entree of Indian-style tandoori chicken or a duck breast covered with Mexican mole sauce. Dessert could be tiramisu (a light Italian cheesecake) or a fat wedge of all-American pie.

In addition to interesting and well-prepared food, Peggy's is a charming place—a long, narrow dining room with bare brick and paneled walls, grapevine wreaths and interesting art. The heart of the restaurant, its kitchen, is in the center of the room, so you can watch the chefs at their work. The decor also shows a bit of whimsy. The door to the women's rest room was obviously salvaged from a local dentist's office and still bears the dentist's name.

When I first visited Peggy's, its logo—a silhouette of a chef on an old-fashioned bicycle—puzzled me. One of the staff members explained. In addition to the restaurant, Peggy's also does quite a bit of catering in the Appleton area. When I looked at the silhouette again, I noticed two details that I'd missed before: The chef has a loaf of bread and a bottle of wine in the basket of his bicycle.

Open 7 a.m. to 11 p.m. Monday through Thursday; 7 a.m. to 1 p.m. Friday; 8 a.m. to 1 a.m. Saturday. Closed Sunday. Breakfast and lunch $; dinner $ to $$. MasterCard, Visa and American Express accepted. Smoking and nonsmoking sections available.

▼ ▼ ▼ ▼ ▼ ▼ ▼ ▼ ▼ ▼ ▼ ▼ ▼ ▼ ▼ ▼ ▼

De Pere

The Union Hotel
200 North Broadway
(920) 336-6131

I n 1918, when the Maternowski family began operating the Union Hotel, overnight guests were a big part of their business. These days, it's the hotel's food that brings fans to the beige brick building with the vintage neon sign hanging over the front door. The hotel's wood-trimmed reception desk is a throwback to the early 20th century, as is its bird's-eye maple bar. If you're a movie buff, those architectural details may make you feel like you're in a film with Rudolph Valentino or Clara Bow.

The Union Hotel follows an odd practice that's still popular at many Green Bay restaurants: Diners are handed menus in the bar and order from that room. A few minutes later, you're led to a table, where rolls and a relish tray are laid out.

The hotel has two dining rooms. The more formal is wallpapered in a bright red print that depicts English country scenes. Personally, I prefer the smaller, narrower dining area, where wooden booths give the room the feel of a coach car on one of the great trains of yesteryear.

Almost half of the restaurant's offerings are steaks, and, if you like a dark crust on your beef, ask the kitchen to pan-blacken one for you. The other specialty is an outstanding pan-fried walleye, though pork and lamb chops are also good. Soups are hearty and homemade and, best of all, dinners come with dessert. Don't miss the homemade pies. They're some of the best you'll find anywhere.

Open 11:30 a.m. to 1:30 p.m. Monday through Friday; 5:30 to 9 p.m. Monday through Thursday; 5:30 to 9:30 p.m. Friday and Saturday; 5 to 8:30 p.m. Sunday. Lunch $; dinner $ to $$$. MasterCard, Visa and American Express accepted. No smoking allowed.

Price Key	
$	Under $10
$$	$10 to $15
$$$	$15 to $20
$$$$	$20 to $25
$$$$$	$25 to $30

Prices are for a single entree. Menus and hours of operation frequently change. Call ahead to avoid disappointment.

De Pere

The Wild Onion
1632 Highway 41
(920) 336-2303

When Hazel Smits bought this restaurant in 1988, she wanted it to be different from most of the other places in the Green Bay area. So she gave the dining room an Australian look. She hung eucalyptus-patterned wallpaper, broke up the room with free-standing rattan screens and dressed the servers in safari jackets. All that was missing was kangaroo steak.

In actuality, the Wild Onion restaurant has never served kangaroo or anything else that's Australian. But there are a few exotic items, like buffalo steaks and alligator tidbits, on the menu alongside more familiar entrees.

Although its atmosphere is a bit unusual, the Wild Onion provides a lot of value for the dollar. Dinners come with a basket of muffins, bread rolls, garlic toast and crackers; three spreads (spinach, cheese and chopped liver); soup; and salad.

House specials include fresh fish and pastry-wrapped beef and chicken. Of the latter, the beef begins with a filet mignon, which is covered with sauteed mushrooms, green onions and Swiss cheese. The chicken is a boneless breast that is covered with mild herb butter before it's wrapped in pastry and baked. Both are quite good. The Wild Onion's dessert tray is practically irresistible. Be sure to try the caramel-custard torte called a Love-um or the strawberry cream torte that combines four layers of white cake with a light strawberry cream filling.

In the summer months, a screened gazebo gives you the opportunity to enjoy the outdoors. It's available to groups of six to eight diners and must be reserved in advance.

Open 11:30 a.m. to 2 p.m. Tuesday through Friday; 5 to 10 p.m. Tuesday through Saturday; 4:30 to 9 p.m. Sunday. Closed Monday. Lunch $; dinner $ to $$$. MasterCard, Visa and American Express accepted. Smoking is allowed.

▼ ▼ ▼ ▼ ▼ ▼ ▼ ▼ ▼ ▼ ▼ ▼ ▼ ▼ ▼ ▼ ▼

Downsville

The Creamery
1 Creamery Road
(715) 664-8354

I f you're a bicyclist and you like good food served in a simple, elegant atmosphere, mark this page in your book. The Creamery in Downsville is a place where you can have it all.

The restaurant is part of a complex that includes a pottery shop and four overnight guest rooms. All are housed in a massive brick building that was home to the Downsville Cooperative Creamery from 1905 until the late 1950s. These days, the building is a block and a half from the Red Cedar State Trail, which is one of the most beautiful bicycling corridors in Wisconsin. It's not unusual, then, to see bicyclists in their bright jerseys seated at the Creamery's tables, especially at lunch.

Brothers Richard, David and John Thomas and their sister, Jane DeFlorin, bought the creamery in 1978. They remodeled and opened the restaurant in 1985. (John Thomas operates the pottery shop.) Surrounded by the picturesque Chippewa River Valley, the Creamery retains its rural look on the outside. Inside, there's a shiny oak parquet floor, attractive wood trim everywhere and beautiful wooden doors.

During the summer, meals are served in the restaurant's screened porch, where diners can watch hummingbirds and butterflies dart among impatiens, nicotiana and other flowers planted just outside. In cool weather, a fire blazes in the fireplace in the inside dining room.

The Creamery's food has an international flavor. At lunch, staff might combine cuisines from around the world by serving a marinated chicken breast with Caribbean black bean sauce, Mediterranean sauteed eggplant and red peppers, Mexican flour tortillas and a Middle Eastern garlic yogurt sauce, all on the same plate. At dinner, there might be roast chicken accented with caraway and apples, or a spicy Senegalese shrimp stew with sweet potatoes and bananas. Summer might bring cold melon or fresh squash soup seasoned with fresh basil. If you're lucky, bread pudding with raisins, pecans and whiskey sauce or sour-cream cheesecake with red raspberry puree will be offered for dessert.

Open 11:30 a.m. to 2 p.m. Tuesday through Saturday; 5 to 9 p.m. Tuesday through Thursday; 5 to 10 p.m. Friday and Saturday; 10 a.m. to 2 p.m. and 4:30 to 9 p.m. Sunday. Closed Mondays and all major holidays. Closed January, February and March. Call for exact spring opening date. Lunch $; dinner $$$ to $$$$. MasterCard, Visa and American Express accepted. No smoking allowed.

▼ ▼ ▼ ▼ ▼ ▼ ▼ ▼ ▼ ▼ ▼ ▼ ▼ ▼ ▼ ▼ ▼

Green Bay

La Bonne Femme
123 Washington Street
(920) 432-2897

Wisconsin has very few French restaurants. One of the best is La Bonne Femme in Green Bay. Once you're past its unassuming storefront, the restaurant feels a bit like Europe, with strategically placed artwork, colored fabric screens and cozy tables.

It feels even more like Europe when you begin sampling chef and co-owner John Swanson's dishes. Each summer, Swanson visits France and, when possible, works in restaurants there. So whether you start dinner with wild boar terrine or escargot with mushrooms, the food is about as authentic as any you'll find on this side of the Atlantic.

For soup, Swanson makes a shrimp bisque flavored with sherry. He also pairs Roquefort cheese with sliced pears and walnuts in an unusual salad. Each night there are special fish and duck dishes, along with wonderful beef, veal and lamb (and, at times, ostrich). Swanson is an expert in desserts. Whether you choose his creme brulee with its crunchy caramelized crust or profiteroles (small cream puffs filled with ice cream and served in an impressionistic swirl of chocolate sauce), the result will be the same: La Bonne Femme will be a restaurant to which you'll want to return.

Open 5 to 9 p.m. Monday through Saturday. Closed Sunday. Dinner $$$ to $$$$. All major credit cards accepted. No smoking allowed.

▼ ▼ ▼ ▼ ▼ ▼ ▼ ▼ ▼ ▼ ▼ ▼ ▼ ▼ ▼ ▼

Green Bay

The Wellington
1060 Hansen Road
(920) 499-2000

In the 12 years since it opened, the Wellington has developed a well-deserved reputation as one of the Green Bay area's most elegant restaurants. Part of that reputation is a result of the restaurant's decor. Sit in the dining room and you'll feel as if you're in the parlor of a beautiful mansion.

But decor is only one ingredient in the Wellington recipe for success. The other is good food. The restaurant changed hands in 1996 and new owners Mike and Nancy Hallada have introduced seasonal menus that emphasize fresh ingredients.

One of the Wellington's specialties is fresh salmon, prepared in different ways depending on the season and the day. A popular preparation is salmon au poivre; the fish is wrapped in a light crust of crushed peppercorns and served on a lemon cream sauce. Another popular dish is salmon *bonne femme*, with shallots, button mushrooms and a rich hollandaise sauce. In summer, there's even a Door County version of the salmon, in which the fish is topped with a cherry and port wine cream sauce and crushed walnuts.

The restaurant's most requested dish is Chicken Marsala, which features chicken breasts stuffed with three types of mushrooms, sauteed and covered with a light veal sauce. The Wellington is also a favorite place for Green Bay diners to enjoy steaks and lobster.

Bread sticks and dinner rolls are made on the premises, and dinners open with homemade spinach and garden vegetable dips, along with cheddar cheese spreads that often are spiked with Cajun or Italian herb blends. Desserts change regularly. Among the best are dark fudge truffles and Door County cheesecake with cherries.

Open 11:30 a.m. to 2 p.m. Monday through Friday; 5 to 10 p.m. Monday through Saturday. Closed Sunday. Lunch and dinner $$$ to $$$$. Separate smoking section available during the week.

▾ ▾ ▾ ▾ ▾ ▾ ▾ ▾ ▾ ▾ ▾ ▾ ▾ ▾ ▾ ▾ ▾

Green Lake

Heidel House's Grey Rock Mansion Restaurant
643 Illinois Avenue
(920) 294-3344

All the ingredients for a memorable meal are present at this restaurant in the Heidel House complex. The Grey Rock Mansion has an attentive staff and a creative menu that changes regularly. The dining room looks like a wealthy family's study, with bookcases lining the walls and a roaring fire in the fireplace on cold nights. And the restaurant offers an idyllic view that's most beautiful in fall when the wooded hills around Green Lake blaze scarlet and gold. If you're looking for a special getaway or want to impress a companion, the Grey Rock is a great choice.

The mansion that houses the restaurant was built in 1949 by Edward Morris. Its design has that simple elegance that was so much in vogue after World War II.

You might start a meal here with wild mushroom strudel or quesadillas filled with brie and apples. Follow up with a Wisconsin classic—an excellent spinach salad with hot bacon dressing and a few diced apples. Entrees showcase some of the best foods of Wisconsin, so there's apt to be well-prepared walleye or lake trout on the menu. In colder months, a North Woods stew made with venison, veal, beef and goose may be offered. The menu, which changes monthly, often features dishes with Italian or Southwestern seasonings, such as grilled salmon with chipotle pepper barbecue sauce or Chilean sea bass with Tuscan white beans and vegetables.

Desserts are made on the premises and elegantly presented after dinner. The Grey Rock has an excellent wine list with a good selection of both whites and reds served by the glass.

Open 5 to 10 p.m. nightly May through October. Open 5 to 9 p.m. Tuesday through Thursday; 5 to 10 p.m. Friday and Saturday; 9 a.m. to 2 p.m. Sunday; and closed Sunday night and Monday from November through April. Brunch $ to $$; dinner $$$ to $$$$. All major credit cards accepted.

35

▼ ▼ ▼ ▼ ▼ ▼ ▼ ▼ ▼ ▼ ▼ ▼ ▼ ▼ ▼ ▼ ▼

Kohler

The Immigrant in the American Club

Highland Drive

(920) 457-8888

Superb food, excellent service and an intimate atmosphere make this restaurant one of the most acclaimed in Wisconsin. Instead of a single large dining room, the Immigrant has six. Each room commemorates a group of settlers who came to the Sheboygan area during the last century: the Dutch, English, French, Austrian, German and Danish. And each is decorated with antiques from the represented country.

Service is formal. Servers wear black coats and ties and work in teams to coordinate prompt delivery of dishes. Entrees are often covered with silver lids that are lifted off the plates in unison.

The Immigrant's changing menu spotlights the best foods produced in the state—Wisconsin beef, veal, lamb, duck and even pheasant, along with the finest fish, including lake trout, salmon, lobster, shrimp and scallops. One section of the menu offers traditional preparations, such as roast loin of elk accented by foie gras; another section lists lighter entrees. At least one (squash-filled ravioli, for example) is created with vegetarians in mind.

The Immigrant's cooking cuts across many national cuisines. One recent choice paired chewy slices of smoked duck breast with delicate but flavorful veal loin. A classic Italian risotto with porcini mushrooms and white truffles and freshly sauteed asparagus tips rounded out the plate.

Desserts are presented on a three-tiered cart with each offering on its own shelf. Creme brulee and baked-to-order open-faced apple tarts can put a fine finish on a memorable meal.

Open 6 to 10 p.m. Tuesday through Friday; 6 to 11 p.m. Saturday. Closed Sunday and Monday. Dinner $$$$ to $$$$$. All major credit cards accepted. Smoking and nonsmoking sections available. Jackets are required for men.

Price Key	
$	Under $10
$$	$10 to $15
$$$	$15 to $20
$$$$	$20 to $25
$$$$$	$25 to $30

Prices are for a single entree. Menus and hours of operation frequently change. Call ahead to avoid disappointment.

EXTRA TIP
Going Dutch

Many of the ethnic groups that settled in Wisconsin have become so assimilated that little trace is left of them. The Dutch are a noteworthy exception. These immigrants arrived in the Badger State in the 1800s and settled along Lake Michigan between Port Washington and Green Bay. The little town of Cedar Grove, about 50 miles north of Milwaukee, keeps Dutch traditions alive with a small museum, an annual festival and a restaurant called **De Zwann**.

The restaurant is decorated with lace curtains and Dutch tiles. While the menu is mostly American, one corner lists Dutch dishes. There's *snert*, a Dutch pea soup that's especially popular in the Netherlands in winter; *metworst*, a Dutch sausage; *croquetten*, the Dutch version of croquettes, made with beef and veal; *gehakt bal*, Dutch meatballs seasoned with lots of nutmeg; and *Zuider Zee*, a platter of flaked smoked salmon served with raisin bread. All are authentic and, with a trip to De Zwann's salad bar and a slice of homemade pie, make a good meal. (Speaking of pie, Dutch apple pie really isn't Dutch at all. It was named for the Pennsylvania Germans who called themselves "Deutsch.")

De Zwann is generally open 7 a.m. to 9 p.m. Monday through Saturday and is closed on Sunday; it's a good idea to call ahead (920-668-8915) and double-check the restaurant's hours before planning a visit. You'll find Cedar Grove 13 miles south of Sheboygan, just west of Interstate 43. The restaurant is located at 115 S. Main St. Look for the sign that has a large white swan on it. In Dutch, De Zwann means "the swan."

▼ ▼ ▼ ▼ ▼ ▼ ▼ ▼ ▼ ▼ ▼ ▼ ▼ ▼ ▼ ▼ ▼

La Crosse

Piggy's of La Crosse
328 South Front Street
(608) 784-4877

Compared to a state like North Carolina, Wisconsin doesn't have a great tradition of barbecuing ribs. But that may be changing. For a taste of good Wisconsin barbecue, plan a stop at Piggy's, one of Wisconsin's premier ribberies. It's located on the banks of the mighty Mississippi in La Crosse.

Pull up in the parking lot, open the car door, and you'll catch the scent of slow-burning hardwood. Piggy's owner Gary Roberts uses tons of it—all cut from the surrounding hillsides and bluffs—to smoke slabs of pork and beef ribs, thick pork chops and tender turkey.

His restaurant is a fun, casual place with a touch of class and a good dose of whimsy. The classy elements are the restaurant's natural oak trim and a magnificent turn-of-the-century oak bar that Roberts rescued from a tavern in Philadelphia. The whimsy is present in the pig theme that runs rampant: Paintings of domestic pigs and their wild cousins hang on the wall, and statues of porcine subjects cram every available nook and cranny.

Ribs aren't the only featured attractions at Piggy's. A few years ago, Roberts added a unit for grilling steaks, and it turns out some of the best-tasting beef in southwestern Wisconsin. A long salad bar features prepared salads and small appetizers, as well as build-it-yourself ingredients. And if you haven't made a pig of yourself by the end of the meal, you may find room for one of the restaurant's most popular desserts: Mississippi Mud Pie.

Open 11 a.m. to 10 p.m. Monday through Thursday; 11 a.m. to 11 p.m. Friday; 11:30 a.m. to 11 p.m. Saturday; 4 to 10 p.m. Sunday. Lunch and dinner $ to $$$$. All major credit cards accepted. Smoking and nonsmoking sections available.

▼ ▼ ▼ ▼ ▼ ▼ ▼ ▼ ▼ ▼ ▼ ▼ ▼ ▼ ▼ ▼ ▼

Traditions
201 Main Street
(608) 783-0200

You say you're looking for a really rich dining experience? How about having dinner in a bank vault?

All you have to do is assemble some friends and call ahead to Traditions, a 36-seat restaurant located in a building that once was the Onalaska State Bank. Restaurant owner and chef Mary Cody has converted the bank's old vault (note the heavy metal door that's left ajar) into an intimate dining room for four. And even if the vault room isn't available, dinner at Traditions can be a great experience, thanks to Cody's knack for creating great dishes.

The menu at Traditions changes every other week, but there are always two appetizers, a soup, five entrees and two desserts. Traditions has a well-chosen wine list that offers many choices by the glass, so you can have a white wine with appetizers and a red to accompany your main course.

Cody's goal is to give diners a chance to taste something they've never had before. It may be a chicken breast stuffed with brie cheese and roasted with a honey almond glaze or black tiger shrimp wrapped in a lemon pepper phyllo dough. She's fond of serving entrees with two different sauces, such as sea scallops rubbed with saffron butter and served over pasta with a cream herb sauce. Salads, which come with dinner, are topped with homemade dressings, such as rosemary vinaigrette and creamy walnut pesto. Soups are also very good.

Whatever you do, save room for dessert. Whether Mary has just made a white chocolate cheesecake with a chocolate crust or has stuffed pears with raisins and currants and is serving them on a vanilla custard sauce, you'll be in for a treat.

The restaurant has been redone in an American Victorian motif. Its walls have been bared so the red brick shows through. With oak tables and chairs, brass accents and bright wallpaper, the building has more charm now than it ever had as a bank.

Open 5:30 to 10 p.m. Tuesday through Saturday. Closed Sunday and Monday. Dinner $$$. All major credit cards accepted. No smoking allowed.

▼ ▼   ▼ ▼ ▼ ▼ ▼ ▼ ▼ ▼ ▼ ▼ ▼ ▼ ▼ ▼ ▼

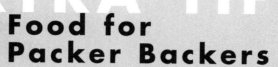

EXTRA TIP

Food for Packer Backers

When you are traveling around Green Bay, it's hard to avoid Packer madness. Folks here are so fond of their champions that Packer posters, bumper stickers and other memorabilia are widely displayed and offered for sale at just about every corner convenience store, and game day traffic around Lambeau Field is legendary. But despite all the extra business that would be available to them on the days that the Packers play at home, many of Green Bay's restaurants stay closed every Sunday.

Two exceptions for a sit-down dinner, the **Union Hotel** and the **Wild Onion**, are described elsewhere in this book. Here are four other places that cater to loyal Packers fans on game days.

Kroll's West, 1990 S. Ridge Road; (920) 497-1111. This restaurant's proximity to Lambeau Field makes it a popular place. Some of the team members themselves have their signatures displayed on the wall. The menu here is a little more extensive than at Kroll's East (listed below), though the owners of the two restaurants are cousins. For those concerned with fat and cholesterol, a fresh tuna plate and grilled tuna sandwiches are offered. There are also Green Bay favorites like fried perch and cheese steak sandwiches. Soups are homemade. To be served, press the buzzer on the wall.

Kroll's East, 1658 E. Main St.; (920) 468-4422. This establishment, the original Kroll's restaurant, has a simpler menu and a 1950s feel. Charcoal-seared burgers, sandwich steaks and chicken breasts are house features, along with chicken, perch, smelt and walleye platters. As at Kroll's West, you have to push the buzzer on the wall for service.

Sammy's Pizza, 2161 S. Oneida St.; (920) 499-6644. A classic stop after a game, Sammy's specializes in thin-crust pizzas loaded with cheese and meat. The house special combines mushrooms, beef, pepperoni, onions, cheese, sausage, kosher salami and green peppers. Meatball sandwiches are quite good, and soups are made fresh daily.

Chili John's, 519 Military Ave.; (920) 494-4624. As its name implies, this restaurant has a reputation for fiery bowls of "red" and great chili dogs. Considering Green Bay's weather in fall and winter, this may be the wisest stop of all.

▼ ▼ ▼ ▼ ▼ ▼ ▼ ▼ ▼ ▼ ▼ ▼ ▼ ▼ ▼ ▼ ▼

Globe Café and Bakery
107 Algoma Boulevard
(920) 235-1111

T he clue to this restaurant's name hangs on the wall of the dining room. It's an old poster for the Odd Fellows, a fraternal order that once occupied the brick building that houses this combination bakery and restaurant.

"The Odd Fellows Lodge was a benevolent fraternity that was founded at the Globe Tavern in England," explains Judy Laing, one of the restaurant's owners. "The Globe Tavern was right next to the Globe Theater, which was Shakespeare's theater. We're right behind the Grand Opera House in Oshkosh, so we named our restaurant the Globe."

And there was another, even more important reason for the restaurant's name when Laing and co-owner Karl Hildebrand opened it in the fall of 1996: They wanted to offer Oshkosh what they call global cuisine—cooking that draws from techniques and ingredients from all over the world.

The restaurant's ever-changing menu reflects that concept. On any given day, diners can try Mexican quesadillas, Italian pastas, Caribbean jerk chicken, hummus and tabbouleh from the Middle East or sesame chicken inspired by the kitchens of China. In addition, several vegetarian items appear on the menu daily.

You might open dinner with a grilled jerked chicken appetizer with fresh mango-tequila dipping sauce and follow with a blackened salmon entree that's topped with poached pear and served over tabbouleh—a salad of cracked wheat, parsley, tomatoes, onions, mint, olive oil and lemon juice. Or you might choose something as simple as a grilled tenderloin steak that the staff has made even more attractive by adding a rich mustard and red zinfandel sauce. All-American dishes like barbecued pork ribs are also quite good at the Globe, especially when they're served with a mashed mix of regular and sweet potatoes.

For dessert, you could try baked custard with a white custard sauce, or, when the berries are in season, fresh strawberry cheesecake.

Open 6:30 a.m. to 9 p.m. Tuesday through Thursday; 6:30 a.m. to 10 p.m. Friday and Saturday; 8 a.m. to 9 p.m. Sunday. Closed Monday. Breakfast $; lunch and dinner $ to $$$$. MasterCard and Visa accepted. No smoking allowed.

▼ ▼ ▼ ▼ ▼ ▼ ▼ ▼ ▼ ▼ ▼ ▼ ▼ ▼ ▼ ▼

Pepin

Harbor View Café
First and Main Streets
(715) 442-3893

When you turn off Highway 35 and drive into Pepin, you may wonder if this small river town is really the setting for one of the state's top restaurants. It seems too small to support such a place. But as you drive into town, you'll notice expensive cars lining the street. If it's a weekend night in summer, you'll also see a lot of well-dressed people sitting outside the Harbor View Café.

Owners Paul K. and Carol Lund Hinderlie and Thomas Rex Ahlstrom bought an old bar on Main Street in 1980, renovated it, redecorated with lots of natural wood, and named it the Harbor View Café. Then they organized their restaurant along the lines of a traditional French establishment, employing local people, many of whom work part-time. The result is a staff that almost seems like it's a family. The servers I've met here have worked at the restaurant long enough to know the dishes well and to make suggestions.

The Harbor View's menu, which is written on a blackboard, lists entrees from around the world. There may be Chilean sea bass with black butter caper sauce or the restaurant's rendition of coq au vin, a French peasant dish of chicken stewed in red wine. Or there might be *kedgeree*, an Indian dish with basmati rice, smoked salmon and grouper. Or, if Paul Hinderlie's in the mood to make it, the café might offer an old favorite called *linguine papalina* that's made with garlic, prosciutto and lots of fresh mushrooms. Desserts could be anything from ginger cake with freshly whipped cream to Georgia walnut pie.

The restaurant does not take reservations, so it's best to arrive early. Seats fill up fast.

Open 11 a.m. to 2:30 p.m. and 5 to 9 p.m. Thursday and Friday; 11 a.m. to 2:30 p.m. and 4:45 to 9 p.m. Saturday; noon to 7:30 p.m. Sunday; 11 a.m. to 2:30 p.m. and 5 to 8 p.m. Monday; closed Tuesday and Wednesday from Memorial Day to Labor Day. Open weekends only from Labor Day to the Sunday before Thanksgiving. Closed between Thanksgiving and the second weekend in March. Open weekends from the second weekend in March until April. Open Thursday through Sunday April to Memorial Day. Lunch $ to $$$; dinner $$ to $$$. No credit cards accepted. No smoking allowed.

▼ ▼ ▼ ▼ ▼ ▼ ▼ ▼ ▼ ▼ ▼ ▼ ▼ ▼ ▼ ▼

52 Stafford
52 Stafford Street
(920) 893-0552

Many of the state's first European settlers were Irish. This tastefully restored inn in Plymouth is a tribute to them. At the heart of the main dining room is a pub so authentic that you'll expect to hear Gaelic as the bartender draws you a Guinness or pours you a shot of John Jameson Irish whisky. And when you search for the rest rooms, look for the doors labeled "himself" and "herself."

And then there's the food. Many Irish sauces are cream-based and rely on spirits for their flavors. So if you order a steak, it's apt to be served with a brandy cream sauce. One chicken entree has Irish Mist liqueur in it to produce a faintly sweet flavor. Corned beef is always on the menu, and it's very good. The restaurant serves hearty soups and breads, and desserts are all homemade.

Because of its proximity to the Northern Unit of the Kettle Moraine State Forest, 52 Stafford is especially busy on fall weekends when tourists from Milwaukee and Illinois take to the roads to take in the fall colors. If you're headed there on a Friday or Saturday night, it's best to make a reservation.

Open 5 to 11 p.m. Monday through Saturday; 5 to 9 p.m. Sunday. Closed on major holidays. Lunch and dinner $$ to $$$. All major credit cards accepted. Smoking and nonsmoking sections available.

Price Key

$	Under $10
$$	$10 to $15
$$$	$15 to $20
$$$$	$20 to $25
$$$$$	$25 to $30

Prices are for a single entree. Menus and hours of operation frequently change. Call ahead to avoid disappointment.

43

Sheboygan

Hoffbrau Supper Club
1132 North 8th Street
(920) 458-4153

Ask a Wisconsinite what makes Sheboygan famous and you're likely to get a two-syllable answer: bratwurst. Over the years, the city has become famous for its brats, which are eaten two at a time in large, chewy Kaiser rolls produced in Sheboygan bakeries.

But there's another culinary trait for which Sheboygan is famous—indoor charcoal grilling. At small restaurants all over town, cooks fire up their charcoal grills about 10:30 a.m. in preparation for the lunch rush and keep the fires covered with sandwich steaks, brats, burgers and chicken breasts all day.

No restaurant takes its grilling more seriously than the Hoffbrau Supper Club, where owner Bob Lauer often tends two grills, one of which is built into the wall. Those grills burn nothing but a special lump hardwood charcoal manufactured in nearby Cedar Grove. It gives grilled meats a clean, natural taste, Lauer says.

You can judge that taste for yourself. Steaks, shrimp and chicken are all masterfully grilled here as are barbecued ribs, which are slathered in a tangy tomato-based sauce. Bratwursts are served in abundance. If you don't want sausage as a main dish, they're also available as an appetizer—grilled over charcoal, cut into pieces and served with brown mustard. The Hoffbrau's menu also lists German specialties like sauerbraten and schnitzel, and there's a nice selection of sandwiches at lunch.

In addition to great grilled meats, the Hoffbrau has one of the biggest and best salad bars to be found anywhere in Wisconsin—you may have a hard time piling everything on one salad plate. Sometimes, Lauer mixes a little fun into the salads. In 1996, when his garden was producing pounds of zucchini daily, he made zucchini pickles. And he couldn't resist adding a touch of yellow food coloring to make them green and gold in honor of Wisconsin's favorite football team, the Green Bay Packers.

Open 11 a.m. to 2 p.m. Monday through Saturday; 5 to 10 p.m. Monday through Thursday; 4:30 to 10 p.m. Friday and Saturday. Closed Sunday except during the Christmas season. Lunch and dinner $$ to $$$. All major credit cards accepted. No smoking allowed.

▼ ▼ ▼ ▼ ▼ ▼ ▼ ▼ ▼ ▼ ▼ ▼ ▼ ▼ ▼ ▼ ▼

Sheboygan
Trattoria Stefano
522 South 8th Street
(920) 452-8455

I f you think Sheboygan's a city that only serves bratwurst and grilled steak sandwiches, you need to head over to this refurbished brick building on South 8th Street. Inside, chef and owner Stefano Viglietti has created a little island of Italy in a Wisconsin setting.

The restaurant's bare brick walls, wooden tables and chairs and terrazzo floor may not be as traditionally Italian as plaster walls and terra cotta accents, but the authenticity of the food more than makes up for it. To start, there are crispy-crust pizzas with a variety of toppings. If it's offered (the menu changes daily), try a *quattro stagione* pizza. The name means "four seasons," and the pizza has four toppings—artichokes, spinach, tomatoes and fontina cheese— along with tomato and mozzarella. If you want the pizza to be really authentic, the kitchen staff will put an egg on top.

Appetizers might include crispy calamari or Italian-style mussels, which are cooked in their shells with lots of garlic. For dinner, thick veal and lamb chops are frequently offered and are usually simply grilled in the Tuscan tradition. (The Viglietti family is originally from Tuscany and retains its ties to the Old Country). Fish dishes are also prepared simply, with a few well-chosen Italian seasonings. And if osso bucco (stewed veal shank) is on the menu, think seriously about trying it. Trattoria Stefano's version is one of the best I've ever eaten.

In addition to regular entrees, the restaurant serves excellent pastas. One version I tried combined fresh Italian sausage and tomato; another used a chicken broth base and added kale and diced fresh Roma tomatoes. For dessert, the Trattoria's version of tiramisu is not to be missed.

The restaurant is usually busy, so it's best to call ahead. If you have to wait, there is a large, pleasant bar where you can enjoy a glass of Italian wine or the traditional Campari and soda.

Open 11:30 a.m. to 1:30 p.m. Tuesday through Friday; 5 to 9 p.m. Tuesday through Thursday; 5 to 10 p.m. Friday and Saturday. Closed Sunday. Lunch $ to $$; dinner $ to $$$$. MasterCard, Visa and American Express accepted. No smoking allowed.

▼ ▼ ▼ ▼ ▼ ▼ ▼ ▼ ▼ ▼ ▼ ▼ ▼ ▼ ▼ ▼ ▼ ▼ ▼

EXTRA TIP

Steak Sandwiches, Sheboygan-Style

No one seems to know how Sheboygan became famous for steak sandwiches. The old-timers say that they've been served in town for as long as anyone can remember.

What makes a Sheboygan steak special?

Well, the steak itself is distinctive. What Sheboyganites call a "sandwich steak" is actually a patty of ground sirloin pressed so hard that it looks like a solid slice of meat. And then there's the cooking. To qualify as the real thing, a Sheboygan sandwich steak needs to be grilled over a charcoal fire in one of the restaurants that maintains an indoor grill. The actual grilling takes only a few moments. Once cooked, the steak is plopped onto a fresh Kaiser roll and condiments are added. "The works" means ketchup, mustard, pickles and onions. One establishment—The Charcoal Inn—also adds a pat of butter. Mayonnaise is available, but you have to ask for it. After it's assembled, the sandwich is wrapped in wax paper that doubles as a plate.

On a busy evening, Schultz's will serve 130 to 140 steak sandwiches and have more patrons than the fancier restaurants in town. It's not unusual for tourists to detour from I-43 and drive 10 extra miles just to enjoy this Sheboygan specialty.

Here are four places that serve Sheboygan steak sandwiches. All are casual, inexpensive spots. Just don't plan on visiting on a Sunday afternoon: Sheboygan is a family town, and most of its eating establishments are closed at that time.

Charcoal Inn North, 1637 Geele Ave.; (920) 458-1147. Open 5 a.m. to 7 p.m. Monday through Saturday; 6 a.m. to 11 a.m. Sunday.

Charcoal Inn South, 1313 S. 8th St.; (920) 458-6988. Open 6 a.m. to 10 p.m. Monday through Friday; 6 a.m. to 7 p.m. Saturday; 6 a.m. to 11 a.m. Sunday.

Schultz's, 1644 Calumet Dr.; (920) 452-1880. Open 7 a.m. to 9 p.m. Monday through Thursday; 7 a.m. to 10 p.m. Friday and Saturday. Closed Sunday.

Terry's Diner, 1426 S. 14th St.; (920) 452-8542. Open 5 a.m. to 7 p.m. Monday through Thursday and Saturday; 5 a.m. to 8 p.m. Friday; 7 a.m. to 1 p.m. Sunday.

▼ ▼ ▼ ▼ ▼ ▼ ▼ ▼ ▼ ▼ ▼ ▼ ▼ ▼ ▼ ▼ ▼

Stevens Point

The Hot Fish Shop
1140 Clark Street
(715) 344-4252

While health enthusiasts may not approve, a favorite way to prepare fish in Wisconsin is to dip it in a made-from-scratch batter and deep-fry it. Served hot from the fryer, the fish is deep gold and crunchy on the outside and steaming hot and sweet on the inside. Few places in Wisconsin do this style of preparation better than the Hot Fish Shop.

The restaurant's history shows that in dining establishments, as in life, things sometimes run full circle. In 1952, Mildred Gramowski opened the Hot Fish Shop, following a formula that had worked well for her uncle, Henry Kowalewski, in Winona, Minn. (The Winona Hot Fish Shop is still in operation.) The batter-dipped, deep-fried walleye and haddock she served made her restaurant a major dining destination in central Wisconsin. In the 1960s, the Hot Fish Shop was purchased by a corporation, which opened a second Wisconsin location in Appleton. That restaurant's popularity declined, and it closed in the 1970s. The Stevens Point Shop reverted to private ownership in 1988.

In 1995, Mildred Gramowski's son, Bob, bought the shop, left its nautical decor intact and brought the menu back to basics. Deep-fried walleye, whitefish and lake perch now top the menu, along with salmon and trout, which are broiled. Full fish dinners come with house potato puffs (French fries are also available) and an unusually zesty cole slaw. For those concerned with calories and fat, almost all the fish on the menu are available broiled as well as fried. There also are six pastas, along with a couple of steaks, just in case someone in your party doesn't like fish. Desserts are all homemade.

Open 4 to 9 p.m. Monday through Thursday and Saturday; 4 to 10 p.m. Friday. Closed Sunday. Dinner $ to $$$$. All major credit cards accepted. Smoking and nonsmoking sections available.

▼ ▼ ▼ ▼ ▼ ▼ ▼ ▼ ▼ ▼ ▼ ▼ ▼ ▼ ▼ ▼ ▼

Stevens Point

The Restaurant
1800 North Point Drive
(715) 346-6010

At the start, the Restaurant feels a little bit like a big city destination. You follow the signs into the Sentry Insurance World Headquarters, then park in a large concrete structure that may remind you of Chicago or New York. But don't worry—the impression doesn't last long. Settle into one of the Restaurant's large upholstered chairs, look out over Sentry's well-tended grounds with their white pines and birch trees, and serenity will quickly sweep over you.

The contemporary dining room with its attractive sloped ceiling and well-chosen artwork provides a visually relaxing atmosphere. It also has some of the best acoustics that you'll find in an eating place, so there is little distraction, even when the room is busy. Adjacent is the I Pagliacci Taverna, which offers outdoor dining in summer and a more casual approach to food. Both restaurants serve Italian dishes, but the Restaurant, which I prefer, is more formal, with linen tablecloths and a more elaborate menu. Entrees here include pasta dishes from both northern and southern Italy, as well as chicken and veal. The house tomato-to-meat sauce has delightful depth. The cream sauces are also quite good, especially over meat-filled tortellini. While it might not be everyone's favorite, spaghetti Caruso (with chicken livers) is a house specialty and is very good.

For those who may not like Italian food, nightly specials feature fresh fish prepared in a number of non-Italian ways. Fresh Atlantic salmon may be cooked in a pecan crust, while swordfish could be sauteed with mushrooms and water chestnuts. Desserts are all done by the staff's pastry chef and can put a great finishing touch on a meal.

Open 4 to 9 p.m. Monday through Thursday; 5 to 10 p.m. Friday and Saturday. Closed Sundays except Easter and Mother's Day. Dinner $ to $$$. MasterCard, Visa and American Express accepted. Smoking and nonsmoking sections available.

▼ ▼ ▼ ▼ ▼ ▼ ▼ ▼ ▼ ▼ ▼ ▼ ▼ ▼ ▼ ▼

Stevens Point

The Silver Coach

38 Park Ridge Drive (Highway 10)
(715) 341-6588

When Jim and Cate Gitter bought this restaurant in 1988, they didn't know what they were in for. Folks around Stevens Point knew that the front section of the restaurant was an old railroad car that had been towed to the site sometime in the 1930s. And Jim Gitter, who is also the restaurant's chef, knew that part of his restaurant's kitchen had been an old box car. But it wasn't until he removed a false ceiling and discovered an elaborate arched stained-glass window that he realized how beautiful the 1905 Minneapolis-St. Paul-Sault Ste. Marie railroad car that made up his front room really was.

Gitter, who studied art at the University of Wisconsin-Stevens Point, worked from dawn to dusk for eight weeks to restore the exterior of the car. He trimmed it in dark wood and refurbished part of it as the restaurant's bar. He also converted two side compartments into small private dining rooms—the two-seat Barney and Smith compartment and the four-seat Glen Flor compartment.

The restaurant's conventionally built 60-seat dining room is behind the rail car. Gitter uses these walls to showcase a few of his own paintings and the works of other Wisconsin artists. In summer, the restaurant serves dinner on an outdoor deck.

Gitter shows his culinary creativity six nights a week in his menu, which runs strong on Louisianian and Southwestern dishes. His chicken mambo, steak Tchoupitoulas and home-smoked back ribs with Louisiana pecan sauce are only a few of the entrees that appear on the menu. When you have dinner at the Silver Coach, be sure to save room for dessert. Gitter makes them all from scratch. His Mississippi Mud Pie, with bananas and creamy homemade chocolate ice cream, is especially good.

Open 5 to 10 p.m. Monday through Saturday. Closed Sunday. Dinner $$ to $$$. MasterCard, Visa, American Express and Discover accepted. No smoking allowed on weekends; smoking section available during the week.

Waupaca

Carnegie's Club Room
321 South Main Street
(715) 256-1031

In 1993, when the citizens of Waupaca vacated their library building, built in 1914, for a new facility, Mary and Larry Gordon and chef and manager Paul Letsch bought it and went to work remodeling it into a restaurant. The finished product is called Carnegie's Club Room, a stylish café that offers a great selection of fresh, well-made meals at reasonable prices.

The restaurant's name comes from the fact that the building, which is on the National Register of Historic Places, was built with a grant from the Carnegie Corp. The restaurant itself is an attractive room done in deep green and cream with lots of natural wood trim. Maple ladderback chairs and antique wooden tables give Carnegie's warmth; contemporary art on the walls adds visual spark.

The center of attention is a small blackboard that lists the daily specials. These range from entrees like thick maple-glazed smoked pork chops served with clove-scented baked carrots and oven-roasted potatoes to turtle stew served in a round loaf of French bread. Or the board might list jambalaya, a richly flavored stew of chicken, ham, celery, green peppers, onions and tomatoes.

Miniature pizzas make nice appetizers or entrees for one person, and there are main-course salads, like grilled chicken Caesar, and hearty soups for those who want to eat light. And at the end of the meal, diners can turn their attention to homemade desserts, such as strawberry-rhubarb or banana cream pie.

Open 7 a.m. to 9 p.m. Monday through Thursday; 7 a.m. to 9:30 p.m. Friday and Saturday; 9 a.m. to 2 p.m. Sunday. Breakfast, lunch and dinner $ to $$. Visa, MasterCard and American Express accepted. No smoking allowed.

Price Key
$	Under $10
$$	$10 to $15
$$$	$15 to $20
$$$$	$20 to $25
$$$$$	$25 to $30

Prices are for a single entree. Menus and hours of operation frequently change. Call ahead to avoid disappointment.

▼ ▼ ▼ ▼ ▼ ▼ ▼ ▼ ▼ ▼ ▼ ▼ ▼ ▼ ▼ ▼

Wisconsin Rapids

The Vintage
3110 8th Street South
(715) 421-4900

There's always something interesting on the menu of this popular central Wisconsin restaurant, thanks to the imagination of Jim Jensen, who owns the restaurant with his wife, Ellen. A graduate of the Culinary Institute of America, Jensen is the restaurant's head chef; Ellen works as hostess. The couple pride themselves on keeping up with the latest culinary trends and offering a changing list of entrees that draws on many different ethnic cuisines.

On any given night, the Vintage's menu shows impressive variety. There may be a New Orleans-style blackened steak, an elaborate Greek salad or an Oriental pasta with a sesame-ginger cream sauce. When indoor grilling became the rage a few years ago, chef Jensen installed a wood-burning unit that turns out tasty meats and fish nightly. His newest addition is a custom-built rotisserie unit that roasts chicken, duck and pork, which Jensen serves with his secret-recipe, honey-bourbon pecan sauce.

What's most interesting is the way in which the chef reinterprets classic recipes. Chicken saltimbocca, for example, is based on a classic Italian veal recipe, but Jensen makes his version with chicken and adds Marsala wine for more flavor.

One of the Vintage's most popular dishes is garlic-crusted New York strip steak. Order it medium rare and the meat will be dark and crusty on the outside and cool and pink on the inside and served with a red wine meat glaze that enhances its flavor.

Desserts give Jensen and his staff one more chance to demonstrate their skills. Sometimes there's brandied apple-blackberry pie, which has a refreshing, tart note. On other days, there's sumptuous white chocolate velvet cheesecake that's served with fresh raspberry sauce.

The restaurant's name reflects its decor: The Jensens have decorated the main dining room with strategically placed wine racks that give it a wine-cellar atmosphere. A nicely balanced wine list ensures that the restaurant lives up to its name.

Open 11 a.m. to 2 p.m. Monday through Friday; 5 to 10 p.m. Monday through Saturday. Closed Sunday. Lunch $; dinner $$ to $$$. MasterCard, Visa and American Express accepted. Smoking and nonsmoking sections available.

Southern Wisconsin

▼ ▼ ▼ ▼ ▼ ▼ ▼ ▼ ▼ ▼ ▼ ▼ ▼ ▼ ▼ ▼ ▼

Bayside

Judy's Kitchen
600 West Brown Deer Road
(414) 352-9998

This charming 32-seat restaurant is a great destination by itself, but it's also a valuable place to know about if you make regular treks up I-43 to Door County. Located in a stone building that also houses a popular pub called the Speakeasy, it is only a block west of the interstate highway. The only problem with stopping at Judy's on your way north is that you might find it difficult to eat a quick meal and then hop back in your car to finish your trip. Judy's is the kind of place in which you'll want to linger, or at least stay for dessert.

Judy Kollmann is the chef who gives her name to this neat little restaurant, and on most nights she's the one who prepares the food. Both the restaurant and the Speakeasy bar are owned by Dean Breul, but in the kitchen Judy's the boss. Kollmann has worked for caterers and restaurants in both the United States and in the Caribbean and emphasizes top ingredients in everything she makes.

For appetizers, Kollmann might serve seared scallops with sauteed sweet potato slices atop a rich Southwestern chipotle chili sauce, risotto cakes with prosciutto, or smoked trout. In the entree department, one of her specialties is chicken Marsala with a delicious wine sauce. Daily specials might include fresh halibut, grilled and then covered with a cool Mediterranean salad of diced tomatoes, onions, garlic and white beans, or steak au poivre, a seared beef tenderloin sauteed with shiitake mushrooms, flamed with brandy and finished with a dab of mustard to form a rich sauce. Even Judy's hamburgers are good—they're made from beef that's ground fresh daily.

Kollmann's desserts are wonderful. Depending on the day you visit, she might have a fresh pear or banana torte, caramel macadamia tart or Door County cheesecake.

Open 11 a.m. to 2 p.m. Monday through Friday; 5 to 9 p.m. Monday through Thursday; 5 to 11 p.m. Friday and Saturday. Closed Sunday and holidays. Lunch $; dinner $$$. MasterCard, Visa and American Express accepted. No smoking in dining area; smoking allowed at the counter and in the bar.

▼ ▼ ▼ ▼ ▼ ▼ ▼ ▼ ▼ ▼ ▼ ▼ ▼ ▼ ▼ ▼ ▼

The Butterfly
5246 East County X
(608) 362-8577

A sign atop the Butterfly, three miles south of Beloit, shouts "Steak" in big letters, but fans of the restaurant often come for a different reason—the nightly special dinners, all priced below $10. On Sunday, roast turkey is the featured attraction. On Tuesdays and Thursdays, it's fried chicken. And on Wednesdays and Fridays, the Butterfly serves a classic Wisconsin fish fry that brings in a crowd.

The Butterfly started out in 1924 as a roadhouse and has steadily grown into a popular dining destination, especially on weekends. The original building was destroyed by fire in 1972, but the Butterfly was quickly rebuilt into a modern, spacious club that seats 180 in the dining room and 96 more on the outdoor deck during the warmer months. The restaurant's sleek interior is decorated in soft pastels and the dining rooms contain large picture windows that look out over the surrounding countryside.

In addition to nightly specials, great steaks (the filet mignon is especially good) and prime rib, the Butterfly offers visitors another attraction—dancing on Friday and Saturday nights when a three-piece combo usually performs in the restaurant's lounge. One visit to the Butterfly will convince you that, in this corner of Wisconsin, "dinner and dancing" isn't dead.

Open 5 to 9:30 p.m. Monday through Thursday; 4:30 to 10 p.m. Friday; 5 to 10 p.m. Saturday; noon to 8 p.m. Sunday. $ to $$$. All major credit cards accepted. Smoking and nonsmoking sections available.

▼ ▼ ▼ ▼ ▼ ▼ ▼ ▼ ▼ ▼ ▼ ▼ ▼ ▼ ▼ ▼ ▼

Brookfield

Café Continental
19035 West Blue Mound Road
(414) 786-9095

S trip shopping malls usually aren't the places where I expect to find fine cuisine. But there's an exception to every rule, and in Milwaukee's western suburbs that exception is the Café Continental. Since 1989, this unassuming little restaurant has been serving well-made breakfasts, lunches, dinners and brunches to patrons willing to brave the busy Blue Mound Road shopping area.

The restaurant has a lot going for it. First, it's a bright, airy place, trimmed in natural oak with light-grained Windsor chairs and with fresh flowers on the table each day. The café's casual atmosphere makes it a convenient spot to visit if you don't feel like dressing up. In addition, chefs Rob and Lisa Ferguson have made the café a showplace for local artwork. The artists' work changes regularly.

The menu is what food experts call café cuisine. The café's basic lunch and dinner menu runs strongest on sandwiches and salads. At dinner, a daily menu lists several entrees. A sizable wine list offers one of the best selections of wine by the glass in town.

Hearty omelets are the stars at breakfast, and at lunch main-course salads like the chicken Caesar or the Cobb salad are especially good. At dinner, there are always interesting chicken and fish entrees and steaks are done simply but very well. However, if I had only one meal to eat at the Café Continental, it would be Sunday brunch. This is a served brunch (not a buffet line) that features such delights as German apple pancakes and Monte Cristo French toast with ham and turkey. Sunday brunch here can be the high point of a weekend.

Open 7 a.m. to 9 p.m. Monday through Thursday; 7 a.m. to 10 p.m. Friday and Saturday; 9 a.m. to 2 p.m. Sunday. Breakfast and lunch $ to $$; dinner $ to $$$. MasterCard, Visa, Diner's Club and American Express accepted. No smoking allowed.

▼ ▼ ▼ ▼ ▼ ▼ ▼ ▼ ▼ ▼ ▼ ▼ ▼ ▼ ▼ ▼ ▼

River Lane Inn
4313 West River Lane
(414) 354-1995

I n 1979, Jim and Claire Marks bought an old building in Brown Deer and transformed it into the River Lane Inn. The restaurant seated 45 patrons and specialized in fresh fish that Jim Marks purchased directly from the coasts. Nightly specials were chalked onto one side of a small board that the waitress brought to the table. The other side of the board listed California wines available by the glass. The restaurant caught on in a big way. Marks has remodeled three times, expanding capacity to 105. And the restaurant's name has become synonymous with great seafood served in a casual atmosphere.

In its early years, most of the fish were prepared simply—sauteed or blackened Cajun-style. That too has changed: Seafood meals at the River Lane are now far more elaborate and are listed on printed paper menus. (The chalkboards are still used for daily specials.) What's offered depends on what is available. If fresh halibut is on the menu, it might be baked in a marvelous macadamia nut crust, while fresh shrimp might be covered with a lively Creole sauce and served over pasta. And instead of the typical small squid that make up calamari appetizers everywhere, one of the River Lane renditions features large "calamari cutlets" pounded tender, sauteed, dusted with Parmesan cheese and covered with tomato sauce.

The inn is famous for three specialties that appear on the menu as often as possible. Cod cheeks and sand dabs (fillets of small Pacific sole) are dipped in an egg wash and sauteed. Blackened fish is prepared in a red-hot skillet and is wonderfully spicy.

Open 11:30 a.m. to 2:30 p.m. Monday through Friday; 5 to 10 p.m. Monday through Saturday. Closed Sunday. Lunch $ to $$; dinner $$ to $$$$. MasterCard, Visa and American Express accepted. Smoking and nonsmoking sections available.

Price Key	
$	**Under $10**
$$	**$10 to $15**
$$$	**$15 to $20**
$$$$	**$20 to $25**
$$$$$	**$25 to $30**

Prices are for a single entree. Menus and hours of operation frequently change. Call ahead to avoid disappointment.

▼ ▼ ▼ ▼ ▼ ▼ ▼ ▼ ▼ ▼ ▼ ▼ ▼ ▼ ▼ ▼ ▼

Cambridge

Clay Market Café
157 Main Street
(608) 423-9616

I have a vivid memory of the first night I visited the Clay Market Café. A friend and I had been walking at Aztalan State Park a few miles way. It was a quiet autumn night, clear and crisp with the scent of burning leaves in the air. We opened the door to the Clay Market Café. Warm air, bright lights and the lively chatter of other diners snapped us to attention. And the delightful smell of basil, garlic and grilling meats set us to salivating. By the time the evening ended, we had enjoyed a fine dinner. I've returned to the Clay Market Café several times since and have enjoyed every visit.

Housed in a 150-year-old renovated grist and lumber mill, the café features antique wooden chairs and tables and Oriental rugs. Windows line two sides of the building, making it an exceptionally bright and pleasant place, especially for breakfast.

There's a distinctive European flavor to many of the dishes served: At breakfast, you might have French *pain perdu* (we call it French toast) or an omelet made with Italian capocollo. The dinner menu for the evening might list grilled steaks topped with Gorgonzola cheese, roast pork loin with an apricot glaze, or small crisp-crust pizzas with goat cheese and Kalamata olives or smoked chicken and mozzarella cheese. Each day the staff prepares an Italian risotto (one contains chicken, shallots, shiitake mushrooms and Granny Smith apples). Pastas are excellent. Homemade desserts, such as ginger custard or 86-Proof Cake (a rich chocolate cake made with bourbon whisky) offer a delightful end note to a meal.

Open 11 a.m. to 8:30 p.m. Monday through Thursday; 11 a.m. to 9:30 p.m. Friday; 9 a.m. to 9:30 p.m. Saturday; 9 a.m. to 8:30 p.m. Sunday. Breakfast, lunch and dinner $ to $$$. Master Card, Visa, American Express and Discover accepted. No smoking allowed.

▼ ▼ ▼ ▼ ▼ ▼ ▼ ▼ ▼ ▼ ▼ ▼ ▼ ▼ ▼ ▼ ▼

Delavan
Fred's Wagon Wheel
3103 County O South
(414) 728-8831

D on't let the exterior of this huge log-veneer building deceive you. From the outside, it looks just like lots of rustic log lodges from the Alleghenies to the Cascades. Walk inside and you'll see how it's different. Apt to be listed on a small chalkboard are oysters Rockefeller, lobster cocktail and conch fritters with coconut sauce.

And those are just starters. Owners and chefs Fred and Mary Hennerley and Patrick Jansen offer an incredible variety of foods ranging from standard steaks and lamb chops to fresh crappies (deliciously sauteed), when they're available. In addition to a staggering list of regular entrees, the chefs dream up several daily specials, many of which are based on fresh fish. Some entrees, like quail and swordfish, are grilled and served with delicate sauces. Others are hearty: veal schnitzel in cream sauce with mushrooms and onions, for instance.

Everything at this restaurant is homemade, from the breads, popovers and crackers to the vanilla ice cream and the hot fudge sauce. If you're lucky, your server will tell you that one of the Wagon Wheel's pies has just come from the oven.

The restaurant's rear dining room is the most comfortable place to eat, though it fills up quickly with fans who drive in from as far away as Beloit and Rockford, Ill. If tables aren't available in the dining room, you'll find it charming to eat off one of the high tables in the bar on a cold day, with a huge fire blazing in the rock fireplace. If you feel like getting in on some fun, take a dollar out of your wallet and a quarter out of your pocket, and write your name and telephone number on a scrap of paper. Ask the bartender for a thumb tack, wrap the whole works up with the tack sticking through, and see if you can get it to stick to the ceiling. If you do it on the first try, you get a free drink. If you get it there on subsequent tries, it will eventually be collected and you'll be invited to the Wagon Wheel's annual customer appreciation day in fall.

Open 5 to 10 p.m. nightly. Dinner $$ to $$$$$. MasterCard, Visa, American Express and Discover accepted. Separate smoking and nonsmoking sections available.

▼ ▼ ▼ ▼ ▼ ▼ ▼ ▼ ▼ ▼ ▼ ▼ ▼ ▼ ▼ ▼ ▼ ▼ ▼ ▼

EXTRA TIP

Fry-day Night Fever

Wisconsin has always had a large Roman Catholic popula-
tion, and the old church rules forbade followers from eating
meat on Fridays. Wisconsinites, especially those living in the
southeastern part of the state, answered that dictate with what
has become a statewide tradition: the Friday-night fish fry.

Thousands of restaurants and taverns offer these dinners
(some also serve them at lunch), and all pretty much follow the
same course: chunks of breaded or battered fish (usually haddock or cod), cole slaw, rye bread, tartar sauce and French
fries. Some continue a German tradition and pair the fish with
potato pancakes. Fish fries range in cost from $5 to $12, with
the price depending on the fish that's offered and whether the
meal is one serving or all you can eat. At some restaurants
you'll find higher-priced walleye or perch dinners, along with
the lower-priced basic fish fry. At many rural locations, fried
chicken is served with the fish.

To find a good fish fry, drive past a restaurant or tavern
around 6 p.m. on a Friday. If the parking lot is full of cars,
chances are the establishment is serving fried fish. The more
cars, the better the fish fry. One of the most famous fish fries in
the state is served in the **Serb Memorial Hall** on Milwaukee's
southwest side (5104 W. Oklahoma Ave.; 414-545-6030). At
card tables set up in the hall and at the drive-up windows, Serb
Hall dishes up a ton of fish each Friday.

Few restaurants take reservations for their fish fries; most
Wisconsinites simply show up, leave their name with the hostess and wait in the bar, sometimes for as long as two hours.
That bar time, some folks confide, makes for a good transition
into the weekend.

Any attempt to compile a complete list of Friday fish fries
would be an enormous undertaking since they're often featured at taverns that don't serve food on the other nights of the
week. Here are six places for you to try. You can call ahead for
hours or just arrive between 5 and 8 p.m., put in your name
and wait at the bar.

The Nite Cap Inn, 227 3rd St., Palmyra; (414) 495-2659.
Great potato pancakes.

▼ ▼ ▼ ▼ ▼ ▼ ▼ ▼ ▼ ▼ ▼ ▼ ▼ ▼ ▼ ▼ ▼ ▼ ▼ ▼

Anderson's, 1474 E. Freiss Lake Drive, Huburtus; (414) 628-3718. Potato pancakes and a pleasant view of Freiss Lake.

The Elias Inn, 200 N. 2nd St., Watertown; (920) 261-6262. Fish, chicken and an interesting array of salads.

M.J. Stevens, 5260 Aurora Road, Hartford; (414) 644-6037. Each dinner includes one to one and a half pounds of cod. Waits are long, but the fish fry is served all day.

Dick Manhardt's Inn, 14000 W. North Ave., Brookfield; (414) 786-5440. Haddock, cod, perch and pike are offered. If you can't decide which one you want, try a combination platter.

Erv's Mug, 130 W. Ryan Road, Oak Creek; (414) 762-5010. A busy bar with an even busier fish fry. Ask for rye bread, if you want it.

▼ ▼ ▼ ▼ ▼ ▼ ▼ ▼ ▼ ▼ ▼ ▼ ▼ ▼ ▼ ▼ ▼

Eagle

Camille's
105 Main Street
(414) 594-5444

You can cover 6,000 miles simply by stepping through the door of this excellent restaurant. Outside, you're in Eagle, which looks like many small towns in Wisconsin. But once you cross the threshold, you'll have the distinct feeling that you are in central Italy.

Owners Randy Piering and Camille DiNicola, who are married to each other, have renovated the former sporting goods store in a magnificent fashion. The plastered walls are painted in warm reddish-brown tones that complement the earthy tiles on the floor. Three spectacular lamps, each carved from a 500-pound block of solid alabaster, hang in the main dining room. There are so many reproductions of classic Italian paintings in the restaurant that you almost expect the ceiling to be painted like the Sistine Chapel. Then you hear Luciano Pavarotti on the restaurant's sound system, and you realize this isn't church.

The art in this excellent Italian restaurant isn't just on the walls. It appears nightly on the dinner plates. Prior to opening the restaurant with her husband, co-owner and chef DiNicola was the pastry chef at the well-known Heaven City near Mukwonago. She has brought her pastry-making skills along with many other culinary talents to the restaurant that bears her name.

One of her best entrees is stracotto. A popular dish in central Italy, stracotto is a stew of beef in red wine. The meat is cooked so long that it falls apart, taking on a rich flavor. DiNicola uses that delicious meat to stuff homemade ravioli, which she then tosses in melted butter and seasons with freshly shredded sage. Her veal medallions are also good—first grilled, then served with a delightful sauce of lemon and Italian *pinot grigio* wine. DiNicola's desserts also demonstrate her culinary talent. Whether it's a fresh pear poached in red wine and served with a scoop of fresh pear ice, or Frangelico cheesecake flavored with hazelnut liqueur, desserts are definitely worth saving room for.

Open 5 to 9 p.m. Wednesday through Sunday, November-April; 5 to 9 p.m. Tuesday through Sunday, May-October. Dinner $$ to $$$$. MasterCard, Visa and American Express accepted. No smoking allowed.

▼ ▼ ▼ ▼ ▼ ▼ ▼ ▼ ▼ ▼ ▼ ▼ ▼ ▼ ▼ ▼ ▼ ▼

Elm Grove

The Elm Grove Inn
13275 Watertown Plank Road
(414) 782-7090

When Norm Ecksteadt and Nico Derni left their posts at a local country club and bought this historic restaurant in 1989, they quickly established it as a top spot in town for Continental food. The oldest part of the restaurant dates back to 1855 and was built as a stage-coach stop and hotel on the plank road from Milwaukee to Watertown. Today, the restaurant's look is Early American, with Windsor chairs and colonial-style wall lamps. But beneath that all-American veneer lies some wonderful French food.

Derni trained as a chef in Nice and excels at classic French cooking. He always features one traditional paté as an appetizer and sometimes makes delicate vegetable terrines that can take the place of salads. Fresh fish is one of the Elm Grove Inn's strongest suits, and Derni usually prepares three or four varieties a night. Depending on what's in season, his menu might list grilled sturgeon on a brandy cream sauce with green peppercorns, grilled swordfish on a light mustard sauce, or Dover sole amandine. In summer, when soft-shelled crab is in season, he prepares the tasty crustaceans in a Provencale sauce that is a specialty of southern France.

Veal is another of Derni's specialties, and it's especially delicious in a morel-cream sauce. Derni also makes a great steak, which he often serves with rich Bordelaise sauce. Derni shows the same creativity with desserts: His mousse tortes and delicate fresh fruit tartlets are especially good.

In addition to the Elm Grove Inn, Derni and Ecksteadt also own and operate the Red Circle Inn, which is also listed in this book.

Open 11:30 a.m. to 2 p.m. Monday through Friday; 5 to 9:30 p.m. Monday through Saturday. Closed Sunday. Lunch $ to $$; dinner $$$ to $$$$$. Master-Card, Visa, American Express and Discover accepted. Smoking in bar only.

Price Key	
$	Under $10
$$	$10 to $15
$$$	$15 to $20
$$$$	$20 to $25
$$$$$	$25 to $30

Prices are for a single entree. Menus and hours of operation frequently change. Call ahead to avoid disappointment.

63

Fitchburg

Quivey's Grove
6261 Nesbitt Road
(608) 273-4900

Have dinner at this restored mansion on Madison's southwest side and you'll get more than a good meal. You'll also get a short course in Wisconsin history.

Some of it will come through the architecture and decor. In 1980, Joe Garton, a former chairman of the Wisconsin Arts Board, purchased an estate on the outskirts of Madison. He restored its main building (a stone Italianate mansion built in 1855) and converted it into an elegant restaurant. The estate's elaborate stable became a casual bar and informal dining spot. And to protect restaurant patrons from frequently inclement weather, Garton connected the two with an elaborate tunnel that took 50 tons of stone to build.

Inside, the restaurant's decor is fascinating. Each dining room presents an aspect of American life in the mid-1800s. The Valentine room, for example, features a collection of "penny dreadfuls"—precursors of modern-day Valentine cards that were popular between 1840 and 1860. In the mansion's music room, sheet music, including an 1852 Stephen Foster original, hangs on the walls.

Then there's the food. Garton and his staff have developed a menu that showcases Wisconsin-produced food, such as trout, duck and veal, in a historical and sometimes humorous way. For example, several of the dishes, which change on a regular basis, commemorate obscure figures in Wisconsin history: One duck dish was named for Charles Arndt, a legislator from the Green Bay area who was shot to death by a fellow legislator while addressing the Territorial Legislature.

The dishes are quite creative and quite good. Smoked trout appears in appetizer tarts and in a salad (with mayonnaise and red onion); duck is roasted and served with apple-cranberry chutney; and venison is grilled and then covered with a whiskey-peppercorn sauce. Dinners come with soup or salad, sourdough bread and fresh muffins.

The Quivey's Grove staff also re-creates dishes from yesteryear. On one visit, the menu featured a steamed chocolate pudding with vanilla sauce, a sweet that was popular in 19th-century America.

Stonehouse restaurant open 5 to 9 p.m. Tuesday through Saturday. Dinner $$ to $$$$. MasterCard and Visa accepted. No smoking allowed.

▼ ▼ ▼ ▼ ▼ ▼ ▼ ▼ ▼ ▼ ▼ ▼ ▼ ▼ ▼ ▼ ▼ ▼

North Shore Bistro
8649 North Port Washington Road
(414) 351-6100

I f you're a fan of the new American bistro movement, this casual yet elegant restaurant in the River Point Village Shopping Center is a must stop. It's everything that an American bistro should be.

Walk in and you might be surprised to know that the space once housed a maze of offices. Owners Michael Tarney, Natalie Soref and Elias Chedid (who also own the fashionable Knickerbocker Café in Downtown Milwaukee and Harry's Bar and Grill on the East Side) softened the rectangular space with several curved partitions. A curved bird's-eye maple panel greets guests in the entryway, and an impressive wall of curved glass panels separates the bar and dining areas. A section of dropped ceiling follows those same curves. Soref and Tarney trimmed the room in light maple and decorated the walls with paintings and bright ceramic pieces. (Smaller art glass and ceramic pieces are displayed in cases built into the west wall.)

The well-planned decor gives the restaurant an easy, casual atmosphere that's carried over to the bistro's creative menu. There are full entrees if you want them, as well as plates of pasta, main-course salads, burgers and sandwiches, and enough creative appetizers to create an interesting meal. Some dishes combine elements of many cuisines. Fried calamari, for example, are rolled in corn meal, then done to a delicious light brown and served with an Oriental plum, ginger and honey dipping sauce. Another appetizer offers a shrimp and corn tamale covered with a creamy garlic sauce. In the pasta department, there are bow-tie noodles with chicken and wild mushrooms and penne pasta made with spicy Italian sausage. For entrees, you might try barbecued ribs basted with dark beer, fresh salmon or a daily special such as pork medallions, sliced from the loin and char-grilled. And if you're a fan of ice-cream desserts, order a Chocolate Godiva, which mixes chocolate liqueur, raspberry brandy and vanilla ice cream. The ingredients are whipped to a peak that towers six inches above the champagne glass in which the dessert is served. Spoon up the mix quickly. It melts fast.

Open 11 a.m. to 10 p.m. Monday through Thursday; 11 a.m. to 11 p.m. Friday and Saturday; 5 to 10 p.m. Sunday. Lunch and dinner $ to $$$$. MasterCard, Visa and American Express accepted. Smoking allowed only in the lounge.

▼ ▼ ▼ ▼ ▼ ▼ ▼ ▼ ▼ ▼ ▼ ▼ ▼ ▼ ▼ ▼ ▼

Genesee Depot

Union House
S42-W31320 Highway 83
(414) 968-4281

Anyone who ate at fine restaurants in the 1970s knows about beef Wellington. Named after the British general and statesman who defeated Napoleon at Waterloo, the entree starts with a piece of beef tenderloin, covers it with liver paté, wraps it in pastry and then bakes it until the pastry turns golden brown. (When it's done right, the beef inside the pastry is a perfect medium-rare.) These days, beef Wellington is hard to find, except at this charming little Genesee Depot restaurant where it's the house special. And it's only one of the delights that appears on the menu nightly.

The building that houses the restaurant was originally the Union House Hotel, which was built in 1861. The restaurant's current owners, Patty and Curt Robinson, renovated the structure and opened it as a restaurant in 1990. The interior is casual, with light pastel tablecloths and tulip sconces on the walls.

Their menu is a four-page newspaper, with pictures and articles on the building's history interspersed with menu items and descriptions. Among the best dishes are pheasant and veal, which is often sauteed with wild mushrooms. The Union House also serves fresh fish, usually grilled and topped with an herb butter or a simple sauce; roast duck, with a port wine and orange sauce; and chicken with raspberry liqueur sauce. Several pasta entrees also are listed.

Desserts range from sweets like "Death by Chocolate," a flourless chocolate cake with chocolate sauce, to lighter, mousselike creations, such as raspberry Bavarian cream. Curt Robinson prides himself on his selection of wines, many of which are available by the glass.

Open 4:30 to 9 p.m. Tuesday through Thursday; 4:30 to 10 p.m. Friday and Saturday; 4:30 to 8 p.m. Sunday. Closed Monday. Dinner $$$ to $$$$$. All major credit cards accepted. Smoking and nonsmoking sections available.

▼ ▼ ▼ ▼ ▼ ▼ ▼ ▼ ▼ ▼ ▼ ▼ ▼ ▼ ▼ ▼ ▼ ▼

Germantown

Jerry's Old Town Inn
N116-W15841 Main Street
(414) 251-4455

Once you get to Germantown, finding this popular rib restaurant isn't all that difficult. All you have to do is drive down Main Street and look for the "pig crossing" sign. While it may not be an official road sign (it's in the restaurant's driveway), it is appropriate: This restaurant serves more than 43 tons of ribs annually.

Ribs are available with three different sauces at Jerry's. The regular house sauce is a slightly smoky but well-balanced tomato-based sauce. Cajun is spicier with a hot-pepper kick. Jamaican has a fruity note and also packs a little zip but isn't overpowering. In addition to ribs, the restaurant offers steaks and Cajun specialties and some excellent smoked chicken. And just in case you have a hard time deciding what to order, several combination plates are offered.

The restaurant's a warm place, with lots of dark wood and subdued lighting. Its delightful decor is 100-percent pork palace. There are drawings of pigs (some flying), paintings of pigs, carvings of pigs, pig figurines and fuzzy stuffed pig toys. The menu pictures an "execu-pig" in a shirt and tie, a dough-boy pig in a World War I uniform and a suave pig-about-town in a blazer. The plasticized bibs that the servers tie around your neck when you order ribs list famous porcine characters such as Bert Porks, Piggy Lee and Ulysses S. Grunt. And if you're still hungry after dinner, you can order Jerry's three-scoop "Pig Slop" ice-cream dessert, which is served in a miniature hog trough.

Open 4 to 10 p.m. Monday through Thursday; 4 to 10:30 p.m. Friday and Saturday; 4 to 9 p.m. Sunday. Dinner $$ to $$$. MasterCard and Visa accepted. Smoking and nonsmoking sections available.

▼ ▼ ▼ ▼ ▼ ▼ ▼ ▼ ▼ ▼ ▼ ▼ ▼ ▼ ▼ ▼

Greenfield

Selensky's Grand Champion Grille

4395 South 76th Street
(414) 327-9100

I n the Milwaukee area, the name Selensky and prime rib have been synonymous for years. John Selensky roasts prime rib using a method that yields
moist, flavorful meat that's almost tender enough to cut with a fork. He has
owned a number of restaurants around Milwaukee and all have been known
for great beef, especially prime rib.

Beef is certainly a big draw at the Grand Champion Grille, but it's not
everything. When Selensky and his wife, Judy, opened the grille in 1994, they
were joined by their daughter, Karen Koltisko, and her husband, John, who are
both graduates of the Culinary Institute of America. The Koltiskos added a
number of items to the menu, including great pastas (the pappardelle with
beef ragu sauce is especially good), crispy appetizer-size pizzas and rotisserie
chickens that are sometimes done with a honey glaze. Several fresh fish dishes
appear on the menu daily. Many of the Grand Champion Grille's patrons still
come for the prime rib, which is prepared in the regular manner or charcoal-
grilled for extra flavor.

The 170-seat restaurant takes its name from John and Judy Selensky's practice of buying grand champion steers at state and county fairs. The restaurant's
look is sleek, with lots of booths and a huge arched window through which
diners can see the work going on in the kitchen.

Open 3:30 to 11 p.m. Tuesday through Saturday; 2:30 to 9 p.m. Sunday. Closed
Monday. Dinner $ to $$$. MasterCard and Visa accepted. No smoking allowed.

▼ ▼ ▼ ▼ ▼ ▼ ▼ ▼ ▼ ▼ ▼ ▼ ▼ ▼ ▼ ▼

The Little Red Inn
4900 Highway 175
(414) 644-8181

I f it weren't for this popular little restaurant, I doubt that anyone except the locals would know there was a town in Wisconsin called St. Lawrence. (The mailing address is Hartford.) As it is, so many people are fond of this unpretentious little restaurant and microbrewery that it would be a mistake to go to the Little Red Inn on a weekend without a reservation.

What makes people flock here is that it's one of those casual places where Wisconsin's German heritage is alive and thriving. The waitresses wear German dresses. The beers, brewed on the premises, have German names like *dunkel hundt* ("dark dog" in German), and the proprietors are named Tim and Sue German. The couple have owned the Little Red Inn for the past 10 years. In 1995, Tim and Sue installed a 3½-barrel brewery upstairs and have been turning out great German-style beers ever since.

Several of the Little Red Inn's well-made entrees are American. The menu also lists German delights. Jaeger schnitzel is a house specialty, and on Sundays, Tim German makes *pfannerle*, a dish that features tender roast beef, pork and veal covered in a luscious cream sauce. It's served in a hot cast-iron skillet with fried potatoes and green beans. Recently, Tim has started using his beers in some of his recipes. One is tenderloin tips, stewed in beer with mushrooms and onions, and topped with a pastry crust. He calls it "a poor man's beef Wellington."

On Friday nights, the Little Red Inn serves a combination chicken and fish fry that includes breaded haddock, crispy homemade potato pancakes, cole slaw and rye bread. Lake perch is also offered and is very good.

Open 5 to 9 p.m. Tuesday through Thursday; 5 to 10 p.m. Friday and Saturday; 4 to 8 p.m. Sunday. Closed Monday. Dinner $ to $$$. MasterCard and Visa accepted. No smoking allowed in the dining room.

▼ ▼ ▼ ▼ ▼ ▼ ▼ ▼ ▼ ▼ ▼ ▼ ▼ ▼ ▼ ▼

EXTRA TIP

Mmm, Custard

Spend some time in the southern half of Wisconsin, and sooner or later someone will start talking about frozen custard. If you've never tried it, you need to know two things: It isn't custard and it's just barely frozen.

Frozen custard is soft ice cream with egg added to enrich its flavor and texture. It's served at a higher temperature than traditional ice cream, so more of the flavor comes out. (It also melts more quickly on a hot summer day.) But don't confuse frozen custard with soft-serve ice cream. While both are made in big machines, usually fresh each day, custard has to be scooped into cones and cups.

While no one keeps official statistics, Milwaukee is probably the frozen custard capital of the world. In the old days, the custard makers guarded their secret recipes carefully and concentrated on one flavor—vanilla. And while they also sold burgers, a few of them wouldn't install French fryers because they believed the odor created by frying would spoil the delicate taste of the custard.

Things changed as many custard stands began offering other standard flavors, such as chocolate, strawberry and butter pecan. The next step was the introduction of exotic flavors, like German chocolate cake and caramel cashew. This trend has swept through the custard stands in Milwaukee, and most now offer three flavors: vanilla, chocolate and the flavor of the day. Printed schedules tell fans when to come for their favorite flavors.

Christmas inspires a flurry of special flavors from peppermint to brandy eggnog. At Omega Frozen Custard, the staff grinds up Christmas cookies to put in the custard on Christmas Eve. And on New Year's Eve, champagne custard is popular.

If you're traveling around the state and want to try custard, look for the blue roofs of **Culver's**, a home-grown chain of combination restaurant/custard stands. Founded in Sauk City in 1984, the operation began franchising in 1989; there are now outlets across Wisconsin and in Illinois, Minnesota and Texas. In 1996, Culver's sold more than 16 million scoops of custard.

For the feeling of how things used to be, head for **Leon's** in

▼ ▼ ▼ ▼ ▼ ▼ ▼ ▼ ▼ ▼ ▼ ▼ ▼ ▼ ▼ ▼ ▼ ▼

Milwaukee at 3131 S. 27th St. (414-383-1784). This custard
stand is classic, complete with fancy neon. Lines form outside
the windows even on cold winter nights.

For a more modern approach, try one of the three **Kopp's**
locations: 18880 W. Blue Mound Road, Brookfield (414-789-
1393); 7631 W. Layton Ave., Greenfield (414-282-4080); or
5373 N. Port Washington Road, Glendale (414-961-2006). The
Greenfield location has a concrete courtyard with pine trees
and a waterfall. The Glendale location is so popular that owner
Karl Kopp has installed a billboard along Interstate 43 that an-
nounces the flavor of the day.

If you're looking for a spot for an informal meal and want
to add custard to it, try **Omega Frozen Custard**, 4695 S. 108th
St., Greenfield (414-425-8520) or **Oscar's Frozen Custard**.
Oscar's are located at 2362 S. 108th St. in West Allis and at
21165 Highway 18 in Waukesha (414) 798-9707.

Kenosha

The Hobnob
277 South Sheridan Road (Highway 32)
(414) 552-8008

Located on the shores of Lake Michigan a mile south of the Racine-Kenosha County line, the Hobnob restaurant has been a popular rendezvous spot between Milwaukee and Chicago since it opened in 1954. Walk into the restaurant and take a look at its white upholstered bar stools, its mirror-tiled walls and its collection of paintings and you may get the feeling that nothing has changed at the Hobnob in 40 years.

But it has.

Look to the right of the bar and you'll see the new terrace room, which overlooks Lake Michigan. Before the new room was built, you had to perch on a bar stool and crane your neck if you really wanted to take in the view. The new room is lined with romantic tables for two that all overlook the lake's wide expanse of blue.

Some of the restaurant's most distinctive dishes, on the other hand, have been on the menu for more than a decade. One of them, garlic bread Uzielli delivers a small loaf of sliced Italian bread with a rich Gorgonzola cream sauce that makes it nearly irresistible. Another house special, steak in a skillet, tops a tenderloin with sauteed onions, mushrooms, green peppers and Dijon butter. Pan-fried chicken and veal scallopini, two other house specials, remain popular with the Hobnob's diners. In addition, fresh fish and pasta dishes appear on the restaurant's list of daily specials.

Open 5:30 to 9:30 p.m. Monday through Thursday; 5 to 10:30 p.m. Friday and Saturday; 4:30 to 8:30 p.m. Sunday. Dinner $$ to $$$. MasterCard, Visa, American Express and Diner's Club accepted. Smoking and nonsmoking sections available.

▼ ▼ ▼ ▼ ▼ ▼ ▼ ▼ ▼ ▼ ▼ ▼ ▼ ▼ ▼ ▼ ▼

Kenosha

Mangia Trattoria
5717 Sheridan Road
(414) 652-4285

These days, authentic Italian trattorias (the Italian word for informal restaurants) are relatively common. But when Mangia opened in the late 1980s, walking into it was a new experience. The atmosphere was that of a casual café, the bread was served with a plate of olive oil for dipping, and if you looked really hard, you could see the glow of the restaurant's authentic Italian wood-fired oven.

For almost a decade, Mangia has been setting the standard for Italian dining in Wisconsin with its simple, flavorful pasta and grilled dishes. Though the restaurant has been expanded and remodeled, it retains its casual, European charm.

For appetizers, Mangia makes wonderful, crispy-crust pizzas. The restaurant's wood-burning oven turns out wonderful fish and chicken entrees, and there are plenty of unusual pasta dishes, including *fettucine della nonna*, which is covered with a well-cooked Calabrese meat sauce. Veal, lamb and fish all find their way into other delicious pasta dishes. Salads and desserts all show remarkable creativity and reflect the seasons. In spring, pasta might feature asparagus, while a dessert might combine strawberries and rhubarb.

Open 11:30 a.m. to 2 p.m. Monday through Friday; 5 to 9 p.m. Monday through Thursday; 5 to 10 p.m. Friday and Saturday; 12 to 8 p.m. Sunday. Lunch $ to $$; dinner $$ to $$$. MasterCard, Visa, American Express and Diner's Club accepted. Smoking and nonsmoking sections available.

Price Key	
$	Under $10
$$	$10 to $15
$$$	$15 to $20
$$$$	$20 to $25
$$$$$	$25 to $30

Prices are for a single entree. Menus and hours of operation frequently change. Call ahead to avoid disappointment.

Kenosha

Ray Radigan's
11712 Sheridan Road
(414) 694-0455

In a world that's constantly changing, it's nice to know that places like Ray Radigan's are still serving dinners the way they used to. The restaurant, which is only a few miles north of the Illinois border on Highway 32, opened in 1933 and has been a popular spot for both Milwaukeeans and Chicagoans ever since. Ray and his wife, Wilma, died in 1994. Their son, Michael, has taken over as chef and owner.

Having dinner at Ray Radigan's is a little like stepping back 30 years. Meals begin with a relish tray of carrots, celery, radishes and olives served crisp on crushed ice. The only tip-off that time has passed comes in the two large pieces of pickled okra that remind you of the Cajun craze of the 1980s. Dinners progress to toasted rounds of French bread, fresh cottage cheese with chives, and kidney bean salad with fresh celery in a mayonnaise dressing. These are served with a basket of bread sticks and packaged crackers. As for entrees, steaks remain a house specialty, but Michael Radigan's kitchen also turns out excellent baked duckling and tender New Zealand venison, when it's available. Full dinners come with salad, hearty soup, an appetizer of marinated herring, fresh rolls, vegetables and dessert. (Banana cream pie is especially good.)

Most dishes are traditional. But that should be no problem. The best part about stepping into the past is that you know how things will work out. And at Ray Radigan's, you'll most likely walk out with a satisfied smile on your face.

Open 11 a.m. to 10 p.m. Tuesday through Thursday; 11 a.m. to 11 p.m. Friday and Saturday; noon to 10 p.m. Sunday. Closed Monday. Lunch $; dinner $ to $$$$$. All major credit cards accepted. Smoking and nonsmoking sections available.

▼ ▼ ▼ ▼ ▼ ▼ ▼ ▼ ▼ ▼ ▼ ▼ ▼ ▼ ▼ ▼ ▼

Lake Delton

Del-Bar Steakhouse
800 Wisconsin Dells Parkway
(608) 253-1861

I f you've ever visited Wisconsin Dells, you know that it's a place with plenty of attractions for children. The Del-Bar Steakhouse, in contrast, is a place for grown-ups—in particular, grown-ups who enjoy good food. Formerly known as Jimmy's Del-Bar, the restaurant has been attracting admirers since Jimmy Wimmer opened it in 1943. Recent additions to the restaurant, which is still in the family, have all been tastefully done by architects who worked with the late Frank Lloyd Wright; the result is a sense of openness that makes for pleasant dining, even when the restaurant is busy—which is just about every night from July 4 to Labor Day.

One of the Del-Bar's biggest attractions is the grand piano in its main dining room. On most nights, there's a pianist, and it's not unusual for the crowd to join in on upbeat numbers. The Del-Bar's popularity also stems from its excellent food. A few years ago, the restaurant introduced a changing menu of well-made bistro specials such as chicken Marsala, veal piccata and cioppino, a spicy seafood stew. For traditionalists, the Del-Bar has long been known for its custom-aged steaks (there are seven on the menu) and for slow-roasted prime rib. If you're in the mood for red meat, try the filet mignon Jim, which is wrapped in bacon and drizzled with Bearnaise sauce.

Open 4:30 to 10 p.m. nightly. Dinner $$ to $$$$. All major credit cards accepted. Smoking and nonsmoking sections available.

▼ ▼ ▼ ▼ ▼ ▼ ▼ ▼ ▼ ▼ ▼ ▼ ▼ ▼ ▼ ▼ ▼

Lake Geneva

The Red Geranium
7194 Highway 50 East
(414) 248-3637

A walk through the Red Geranium tells you immediately how popular a place it is. You walk through one dining room and into another. Walk through the next one and there's another. And another after that. Wonder why? The Red Geranium, which was opened 12 years ago by the Swatek family, has become so popular that the owners have had to keep adding new dining areas.

The main building of the restaurant was originally a sprawling home and later was converted to an antique shop. The Swateks—Lyle, Audrey and their son and daughter-in-law Mark and Phoebe—bought the building and renovated it into a restaurant in 1985. Each of the restaurant's dining rooms is decorated in a bright country motif. The walls of the dining rooms are covered with red geranium wallpaper.

The menu has something for every taste. Like thick steaks or grilled seafoods? There's an indoor grill that imparts the flavor of charcoal even during the coldest months of the year. Want something fancier? Try duck with Door County cherry sauce or thick lamb chops with a delightful house mint-mustard sauce. These entrees are all very good, and the meal becomes even better when a server comes to your table with a cookie sheet loaded with freshly made buttermilk biscuits. I dare you to resist them. And if you're not in the mood for dinner, keep the Red Geranium in mind for Sunday brunch, which is served until 3 p.m.

Open 11:30 a.m. to 2:30 p.m. Monday through Saturday; 5 to 9 p.m. Monday through Thursday; 5 to 10:30 p.m. Friday and Saturday; 11:30 a.m. to 9 p.m. Sunday. Lunch $; dinner $$ to $$$$$. All major credit cards accepted. Smoking and nonsmoking sections available.

▼ ▼ ▼ ▼ ▼ ▼ ▼ ▼ ▼ ▼ ▼ ▼ ▼ ▼ ▼ ▼ ▼ ▼ ▼ ▼

EXTRA TIP

A World-
Class Diner

In the spring of 1996, when President Bill Clinton and German Chancellor Helmut Kohl held a mini-summit in Downtown Milwaukee, the local news media found itself asking one question day after day:

Where would the two leaders eat lunch?

Since, for security reasons, such decisions aren't announced ahead of time, speculation grew. Surely, Chancellor Kohl, who weighs close to 300 pounds, would want a German meal, some experts said. Others noted that Kohl likes Italian food, and thought he might pick a popular pasta place. Still others thought that the men would choose one of the fancier spots in town. Restaurateurs reported advance visits by Secret Service and German security teams. Some bought special ingredients or made cakes in anticipation of a visit.

The world leaders ended up at a 1950s revival restaurant called **Miss Katie's Diner.**

Long a popular spot with the Marquette University crowd, Miss Katie's (1900 W. Clybourn St.; 414-344-0044) was built in the 1980s but looks like restaurants did four decades ago. And at night, the tables in front of the picture windows on the south side of the building come with a delightful view of the lights twinkling in the Menomonee River Valley.

Miss Katie's is well worth a stop if you're in the mood for a casual meal. The diner serves blue plate specials, along with Kansas City-style ribs and Italian dishes. It's also known for its hearty breakfasts, like scrambled eggs with Italian sausage and toasted Italian bread.

When you visit, be sure to look for the picture of the staff standing with Bill and Helmut, and ask your server about the day that made the restaurant famous. And if you feel like it, order the appetizer platter of riblets, mozzarella sticks and other delicacies. It was served to the two leaders, which makes it the food of international diplomacy.

▼ ▼ ▼ ▼ ▼ ▼ ▼ ▼ ▼ ▼ ▼ ▼ ▼ ▼ ▼

Madison

Blue Marlin Restaurant and Raw Bar

101 North Hamilton Street

(608) 255-2255

This fashionable restaurant just off the Capitol Square offers glittering testimony to America's growing love affair with fresh fish. Just about everything on the Blue Marlin's menu is seafood. Even the one steak that is offered—Australian carpetbag steak—is stuffed with fresh oysters.

The restaurant's decor includes marble inlays on the walls, pictures of battleships in the rear of the restaurant and stylish chairs and tables. Together, these design elements give the restaurant a chic urban feel that translates into a lively atmosphere, especially in the evening.

The Blue Marlin's menu changes with the availability of fresh fish in the local markets, and the restaurant's customers don't seem to mind a bit. Sometimes the best fish available is Chilean sea bass; other nights the specials might include fresh tuna or the restaurant's namesake, blue marlin. One of the Blue Marlin's signature dishes is its seafood pasta—linguine covered with a tomato sauce with scallops, shrimp, calamari, green-lipped mussels, fresh fish and yellow and red peppers. With a fresh chunk of chewy sourdough bread, it makes a magnificent meal. Entrees are usually grilled and served with flavored butters or light sauces. Alaskan halibut, for example, may be grilled and covered with a light sauce of olive oil, horseradish, lime juice, shallots, garlic and honey—a simple and delicious dish.

Dinners come with soup and either tossed or Caesar salad, served European-style after the entrees. For dessert, cheesecake is a good bet. The Blue Marlin has an extensive selection of white wines, many of which are served by the glass. And the Blue Marlin has another distinction: It's one of the few elegant restaurants in Madison that's open on Sunday night.

Open 11:30 a.m. to 2:30 p.m. Tuesday through Friday; 5:30 to 10 p.m. Tuesday through Saturday; 5:30 to 9 p.m. Sunday. Closed Mondays and the first week of January. Lunch $ to $$; dinner $$$ to $$$$$. All major credit cards available. No smoking allowed.

▼ ▼ ▼ ▼ ▼ ▼ ▼ ▼ ▼ ▼ ▼ ▼ ▼ ▼ ▼ ▼ ▼

Madison
Deb & Lola's
227 State Street
(608) 255-0820

The first mistake you might make at this fashionable State Street restaurant is to think that Deb and Lola are sisters. The two owners are related, but it's by marriage. The "Deb" in the title is the nickname of chef Brian Boehm, who owns the restaurant with "Lola," his wife Angela Kinderman.

Since it opened in 1993, Deb and Lola's has been delighting its patrons with unusual dishes, many of which have a decidedly Southwestern flavor. Black bean soup and free-range chicken tacos have been two of the restaurant's most popular offerings. But to say that this restaurant is strictly Southwestern would be a little too limiting. Boehm has always been one to experiment with ingredients and deliver culinary surprises, like German spaetzel noodles made with rich Wisconsin cheddar cheese or grilled polenta with Gorgonzola cheese and spicy Habanero chilis. Most recently, Boehm has been exploring regional Mexican cuisine and introducing some of its ingredients into the dishes that the chic restaurant offers nightly, such as grilled salmon with a pineapple, tamarind and smoky chili sauce or grilled chicken enchiladas with Oaxacan mole sauce.

Desserts at Deb & Lola's range from light dishes, such as traditional flan, to heavy chocolate caramel creations. In the past, Deb has even been known to put mild chiles in a chocolate cake, with delicious results.

And in case you're wondering how the chef and co-owner got his nickname, the story goes like this: At one point in his career, Boehm was working in a kitchen with several other Brians. In an effort to keep their identities straight, the Brians resorted to nicknames. "Deb" came from Brian's habit of occasionally indulging in a brand of snack cakes called "Little Debbie's." Angela got her nickname from Brian, who told her she dressed like singer and dancer Lola Falana.

Open 5 to 10 p.m. Monday through Saturday. Closed Sunday. Dinner $$ to $$$$. MasterCard and Visa accepted. No smoking in the dining area.

Madison

Fyfe's Corner Bistro
1344 East Washington Avenue
(608) 251-8700

When it was first built at the turn of the century, the large beige brick building on busy East Washington Avenue housed a farm implement store. After almost a century, the building is still connected with food: It's become a popular American bistro.

In France, bistros are casual places, where diners choose from a large selection of dishes and assemble a meal one course at a time. Fyfe's Corner Bistro is the same sort of place, with a varied menu of steaks, salads, pastas and appetizers. It's also a great place to get away from the world. There's enough space between the white-clothed tables to give diners privacy, and its beige walls and subdued lighting create a sheltered spot from the storms of a busy world.

The menu's broad enough that anyone can create a meal to satisfy his or her personal taste. In the appetizer department, there's a baked brie with fresh sourdough bread and thin crostini brushed with olive oil and grilled to create a wonderful crustiness. If you're a pasta lover, you'll enjoy entrees like fettuccini with shrimp and scallops or with chicken, which both rely on a rich cream sauce to tie their flavors together. Other entrees include Black Angus steaks and oven-roasted pork tenderloin, which is served in attractive slices fanned out atop a rich port wine-cranberry sauce. Fresh vegetables and garlic mashed potatoes accompany both. For dessert, try flourless chocolate cake, which is made with dark Belgian chocolate. It's so dense and rich that it tastes almost like chocolate candy.

Open 11 a.m. to 2 p.m. Monday through Friday; 5:30 to 10 p.m. nightly. Sunday brunch served 10 a.m. to 2 p.m. Lunch and dinner $ to $$$. MasterCard, Visa and American Express accepted. No smoking allowed in the dining area.

Price Key

$	Under $10
$$	$10 to $15
$$$	$15 to $20
$$$$	$20 to $25
$$$$$	$25 to $30

Prices are for a single entree. Menus and hours of operation frequently change. Call ahead to avoid disappointment.

▼ ▼ ▼ ▼ ▼ ▼ ▼ ▼ ▼ ▼ ▼ ▼ ▼ ▼ ▼ ▼ ▼

Madison

Kabul Restaurant

541 State Street
(608) 256-6322

Take a look at the sign for this busy State Street restaurant, and you'll notice a subhead that says "Afghanistan and Mediterranean Cuisine." On a map of the world, the distance between Afghanistan and the Straits of Gibraltar is almost halfway around the world. But Kabul's menu covers the territory well, listing delights such as Afghan kebabs just above Moroccan couscous. The best part of it all is that the food served in the casual 60-seat restaurant is reasonably priced and very good. Owned by Ghafoor and Saboor Zafari, Kabul attracts both university students and visitors who enjoy ethnic foods.

Meals begin with a basket of flat Afghan bread and include a choice of soup or salad. Salads are respectable but not as interesting as the house soup: *mashawa*, a fragrant mix of lamb, chicken, chick peas, kidney beans, split peas and rice, with a dollop of fresh yogurt swirled into it at the last minute. Ask Ghafoor Zafari about the soup and he'll tell you it actually tastes better if it's refrigerated overnight and reheated the next day. Then he'll smile and say, "The problem is we never have any left at the end of the night."

For entrees, traditional Afghan beef kebabs alternate cubes of marinated tenderloin with cherry tomatoes, green peppers and onions. Kabul kebabs are similar but substitute chunks of chicken, salmon and swordfish for the beef. Two other outstanding offerings are Moroccan lemon chicken made with potatoes, onions, olives, pimento and specially preserved lemons (preserving gives the lemons an intense flavor), and couscous, a hearty North African stew that's served over tiny pastalike grains of wheat.

Open 11 a.m. to 10:30 p.m. Monday through Thursday; 11 a.m. to 11 p.m. Friday and Saturday; 11 a.m. to 10 p.m. Sunday. Lunch $; dinner $ to $$. All major credit cards accepted. No smoking allowed.

81

Madison

L'Etoile

25 North Pinckney Street
(608) 251-0500

I f you're looking for one restaurant that is quintessentially Wisconsin, you will have to visit this charming, second-story establishment overlooking the State Capitol. The restaurant's owner and chef, Odessa Piper, has been a leader in showcasing state-produced foods since she opened her restaurant in the late 1970s.

L'Etoile's menu, which is rewritten each week, routinely features locally grown fruits and vegetables, locally raised meats and locally made cheeses, all blended with a heavy helping of Piper's own culinary genius.

While the meats, fish, vegetables and berries spring from Wisconsin roots, a dinner at L'Etoile has some European touches. Salads can be served before or after entrees (your choice), and a nice selection of aperitifs and well-chosen wines is offered.

Like all great restaurants, L'Etoile's menu follows the seasons. So in spring you might enjoy a delicate sauté of wild mushrooms and organically grown asparagus; in fall, you might end your meal with a puff pastry "purse" filled with a sweet hickory-nut filling.

If you do have a problem at L'Etoile, it may be trying to select your entree from a long list of seductive selections. Lean Wisconsin pork loin usually is featured, along with salmon and locally raised trout. Free-range chicken also makes a flavorful entree. Side dishes, like potato-zucchini pancakes and homemade succotash, are just as interesting as the entrees. All those extra touches add up to make a dinner at L'Etoile one of the most memorable meals anywhere in the state.

Open 6 to 8:45 p.m. Monday through Thursday; 5:30 to 9:30 p.m. Friday; 5 to 9:30 p.m. Saturday. Closed Sundays and major holidays. Dinner $$$ to $$$$. Visa, MasterCard and Diner's Club accepted. Smoking not allowed in the dining area.

▼ ▼ ▼ ▼ ▼ ▼ ▼ ▼ ▼ ▼ ▼ ▼ ▼ ▼ ▼ ▼

Madison
Pasta Per Tutti
2009 Atwood Avenue
(608) 242-1800

I n the restaurant business, bread is a lot like a business card. It introduces the restaurant's food, and when it's good it can win diners over before they take their first bite of their entree. For the first year that Joe Sandretti operated Pasta Per Tutti on Madison's East Side, he bought Italian bread from a local bakery. Then he decided to bake his own. He began making what is some of the best country-style Italian bread available on this side of the Atlantic. It has big holes, it's chewy, and it has a wonderful flavor and fragrance. And it's only one of the treats available at Pasta Per Tutti.

The restaurant's decor, like many of its dishes, is simple, with only a few well-chosen works of art dotting the vintage brick walls. The menu is also simple, with several basic pasta dishes forming its backbone. There are old familiars like spaghetti with meatballs and pasta carbonara. *Cioppino*, a seafood stew that was originally a special, has moved to the permanent menu along with chicken saltimbocca. Pasta with pesto, made with fresh basil and plenty of garlic, is another of Pasta Per Tutti's strong suits. There's also an Italian version of a mixed grill, which features lamb, sausage and chicken, all marinated in olive oil with fresh rosemary. It's served with a skewer of seasoned grilled vegetables.

For dessert, it's hard to beat the restaurant's great tiramisu, which is rich with the flavor of mascarpone cheese and coffee liqueur.

Open 5 to 9 p.m. Sunday through Thursday; 5 to 10 p.m. Friday and Saturday. Dinner $$ to $$$. Visa and MasterCard accepted. No smoking allowed.

▼ ▼ ▼ ▼ ▼ ▼ ▼ ▼ ▼ ▼ ▼ ▼ ▼ ▼ ▼ ▼ ▼

Madison

Smoky's Club
3005 University Avenue
(608) 233-2120

Madison is one of Wisconsin's most exciting restaurant towns. With its strong national reputation, the University of Wisconsin attracts students from all over the world. Some of them never leave and open restaurants serving their native cuisine. Other Madison restaurateurs are quick to spot national trends and capitalize on them. But in the midst of all the exciting new restaurants that seem to open in Madison every month, there's Smoky's Club, a spot that's been serving great steaks since its founder Leonard (Smoky) Schmock opened the club in 1952.

Part of the fun of Smoky's is its rummage-sale decor. The labyrinthine 145-seat restaurant has four dining rooms that sprawl in all directions from a central bar. The decorations on the walls run from reprints of movie posters for *The Wizard of Oz* to antique farm implements. A whimsical hodgepodge of collectibles dangles from the ceiling and hangs from the walls. Depending on where you're seated, a plastic tyrannosaurus rex dinosaur, a battered tuba, an ancient leather football helmet or a dried puffer fish might dangle over your head. The Schmock family (these days, Smoky's sons, Tom and Larry, take care of most day-to-day operations) gathered most of the decorations, though regular customers have been known to bring in such items as inflatable pigs and stuffed sailfish.

Smoky's aged steaks, and especially its filet mignon and New York strip sirloin, are some of the finest you'll find anywhere. They're broiled on a thick, flat steel grill at a temperature so high that the meat is seared and its juices are sealed in. In addition to marvelous beef, Smoky's also serves great fried chicken and old-fashioned, hand-breaded shrimp. There's also a vegetable stir-fry for the vegetarian contingent.

Dinners start with a small stoneware crock of iced vegetables—carrot sticks, celery, green onions and radishes—along with a bowl of cottage cheese and a bread basket containing Smoky's own homemade garlic toast. Entrees arrive with either French fries or hash brown potatoes, the latter fried in small pans, then turned out onto plates at the table. With their beautifully browned tops, the molded potatoes look and taste like inch-thick potato pancakes.

Like its main menu, Smoky's dessert list is simple. If you have any room left or need a sweet finish, you'll have to settle for a sundae.

Open 5 to 10 p.m. Wednesday through Saturday and Monday. Closed Sunday, Tuesday and all major holidays. Dinner $ to $$$. Credit cards not accepted. No smoking allowed in the dining area.

▼ ▼ ▼ ▼ ▼ ▼ ▼ ▼ ▼ ▼ ▼ ▼ ▼ ▼ ▼ ▼

Tornado Club Steak House
116 South Hamilton Street
(608) 256-3570

Henry Doane long had dreamed of opening a 1950s-style steak house within the shadow of the Wisconsin State Capitol. When he took over Larry's Fish and Steak House (formerly Crandall's) in 1996, he found much of his work already done for him. First opened in 1958, with knotty pine walls and exposed wooden trusses, the eatery looked like a place that time had forgotten. Doane added some vinyl booths and a healthy dose of neon and the Tornado Club Steak House was born.

A talented chef who was part of the team that developed the Blue Marlin (also listed in this book), Doane knows what it takes to draw a crowd in Madison. He's put six steaks at the top of the menu, just as restaurateurs would have done in the 1950s. But a few other touches are decidedly postmodern. At the beginning of a meal, diners face an odd variation of a 1950s relish tray: Olives, celery sticks, carrots, radishes and a pickle spear are arranged in a surrealistic bouquet in a tall glass tumbler. And poultry, venison and rabbit are featured along with crab legs, broiled shrimp and pan-fried walleye.

One of the Tornado Club's most popular appetizers is its version of coquilles St. Jacques. Three huge scallops are poached in white wine, finished with heavy cream and then served in a shell atop attractively piped mashed potatoes. Frog legs and oysters also are available as meal starters. For entrees, it's hard to beat the filet mignon, which is peppered and then grilled over a flame hot enough to create a tasty crust. Pan-roasted duck breast is served with a port wine-currant sauce.

If you've a taste for traditional beef accompaniments, Yorkshire pudding is available as a side dish. So are green beans, Brussels sprouts and fresh asparagus. Even the breads here are interesting, including homemade bread sticks, fresh baking powder biscuits and whole wheat bread still hot from the oven.

Make sure to reserve room for dessert—perhaps a thick, three-layer German chocolate cake or a lovely double-crust pie filled with fresh peaches.

Open 5:30 to 10 p.m. Tuesday through Saturday, 5:30 to 9 p.m. Sunday. Dinner $$ to $$$$$. MasterCard, Visa and Discover accepted. No smoking allowed in the dining room.

▼ ▼ ▼ ▼ ▼ ▼ ▼ ▼ ▼ ▼ ▼ ▼ ▼ ▼ ▼ ▼

Madison
Wilson Street Grill
217 South Hamilton Street
(608) 251-3500

Located within a few blocks of the State Capitol, this stylish restaurant has been one of Madison's trendiest places to eat since it opened in 1988. Part of its appeal is visual. The restaurant's dining room has clean horizontal lines, natural wood trim and expertly chosen artwork. There's an outdoor balcony that's used in summer.

And that's only decor. The Grill's greatest asset is its creative menu, which features many of the foods Wisconsinites love served in new and exciting ways.

The menu changes regularly but always offers a delightful blend of the new and the nostalgic. Take sausage, which has always been popular in a state with a strong German tradition. Most places put it in a roll and pile on toppings. At the Wilson Street Grill, the sausage might be specially made of lean veal, then grilled and served with a selection of mustards from around the Midwest. A specially made lamb sausage tops one of the Grill's small, crispy pizzas.

Pork chops are thick, and grilling brings out their flavor. They often come with Wisconsin touches, such as a chunky sauce of Door County cherries and hearty pinot noir wine. The Wilson Street Grill also does an outstanding job with fresh fish, which is grilled and then served with a creative sauce or mayonnaise. And don't be surprised to see some Asian influences in dishes such as sesame chicken and shrimp, which is served with cold sesame noodles and crunchy Chinese cabbage.

Before you order, think seriously about dessert, which could be as exotic as a selection of three tiny custards or as old-fashioned as moist chocolate layer cake served with caramel sauce, pecans and banana ice cream.

Open 11 a.m. to 2 p.m. Monday through Friday; 5 to 9:30 p.m. Tuesday through Saturday. Closed Sunday. Lunch $; dinner $ to $$$. MasterCard and Visa accepted. No smoking allowed in the restaurant; smoking allowed on the terrace, which is open in summer.

▼ ▼ ▼ ▼ ▼ ▼ ▼ ▼ ▼ ▼ ▼ ▼ ▼ ▼ ▼ ▼ ▼

Mayville
The Audubon Inn
45 North Main Street
(920) 387-5858

One of Wisconsin's greatest nature shows begins in late summer at Horicon Marsh, about 60 miles northwest of Milwaukee, where thousands of Canada geese make a stopover on their way south. The huge waves of birds in their characteristic V formation draw thousands of spectators each year. Birds are also a big draw at the Audubon Inn in nearby Mayville. But these birds are depicted in stained-glass windows and on the walls of the classy restaurant.

Like its sister inn, 52 Stafford (also listed in this book), the Audubon Inn is an attractive restoration of a vintage building, the Beaumont Hotel, which was built in Mayville by Jacob and Anna Mueller in 1896. A high chair rail and oak wainscoting circle the room beneath Victorian-inspired print wallpaper. Copies of John J. Audubon's famous prints are elegantly framed and hang on the walls. Dividing the dining room and the bar is a large etching of an egret, and set into the brilliantly colored stained-glass windows in the front of the room are the images of some of Wisconsin's favorite birds: a red-headed woodpecker, bluebird, bobwhite quail, Baltimore oriole, robin, blue jay, cedar waxwing, cardinal, purple martin, red-winged blackbird, goldfinch, and black and white warbler.

Besides being a beautiful place for a meal, the inn's food is very good. The menu changes seasonally. Among the most popular dishes are rack of lamb, roast duck and chicken specials, such as boneless chicken breast rolled in crushed hazelnuts, and Chicken Calvados and asparagus (made with French apple brandy). All the restaurant's breads and desserts are baked on the premises; cheesecakes and cream tortes are especially good.

Open 5 to 10 p.m. Monday through Saturday. Closed Sunday. Dinner $$$ to $$$$. All major credit cards accepted. No smoking allowed.

▼ ▼ ▼ ▼ ▼ ▼ ▼ ▼ ▼ ▼ ▼ ▼ ▼ ▼ ▼ ▼ ▼

Mequon

Boder's on the River

11919 North River Road
(414) 242-0335

I n 1929, when the Boder family opened its restaurant along the Milwaukee River, going there to eat meant a long drive in the country. Now, with modern freeways and faster cars, the drive to Boder's from downtown Milwaukee takes half an hour or less. And the restaurant's property, which once was the site of a camp for underprivileged children, is now in a suburban setting.

While the neighborhood may have changed, Boder's has stayed in the family. And it's still serving some of the same dishes that founders John and Frieda Boder offered their customers during the last days of the Roaring Twenties.

The restaurant specializes in simple, straightforward entrees such as roast duck, sauteed veal cutlets, baked fish and chicken, and hand-breaded shrimp, served with the restaurant's trademarks—homemade muffins, a fresh fruit plate and corn fritters dusted with powdered sugar. (If all those extra dishes seem like too much, you can choose one of the lighter meals.)

Sundays are big days at Boder's. Both regular lunch dishes and special brunch items are available. Brunches include platters of scrambled eggs, chicken livers, bacon and ham. A small entree, such as chicken Kiev or salmon steak, follows.

Open 11:30 a.m. to 2 p.m. Tuesday through Sunday; 5:30 to 8 p.m. Tuesday through Thursday; 5:30 to 9 p.m. Friday and Saturday; 4 to 7 p.m. Sunday. Closed Monday. Lunch $ to $$; dinner $$ to $$$$$. All major credit cards accepted. No smoking allowed.

▼ ▼ ▼ ▼ ▼ ▼ ▼ ▼ ▼ ▼ ▼ ▼ ▼ ▼ ▼ ▼

Mequon

The Riversite
11120 North Cedarburg Road
(414) 242-6050

I n the late 1980s, with his River Lane Inn going strong, Jim Marks decided he wanted to do something more upscale. The Riversite was the result, and since it opened it's been one of the best formal restaurants in Wisconsin.

The restaurant's elegant dining room features an expansive wood cathedral ceiling with glittering chandeliers, a small forest of plants and a 10-foot-high, turn-of-the-century breakfront that Marks found in the basement of a woodworking shop. A few of the restaurant's tables overlook the Milwaukee River.

But while the restaurant's interior is attractive, its menu is what keeps patrons coming back. Changing monthly, the menu emphasizes meats and seasonal fare. One spring, for example, the Riversite included fresh raspberries in two wonderfully creative sauces: Guinea hen was served with a sharp raspberry-rhubarb sauce, and salmon steak came with a sweet raspberry and port-wine sauce. Rack of lamb and veal are always good choices from this menu, as are the occasional exotic entrees. On one visit, the Riversite featured a terrine of wild boar; on another, it offered grilled antelope. The fresh fish is also very good.

The Riversite's appetizers and desserts are as fun to look at as they are delicious to eat. A meal might begin with an elaborate pastry pouch filled with sausage and crayfish, and end with a cold dark-chocolate marquise atop a rich vanilla custard sauce.

Open 5 to 10 p.m. Monday through Saturday. Closed Sunday. Dinner $$ to $$$$. MasterCard, Visa and American Express accepted. Smoking and nonsmoking sections available.

Price Key

$	Under $10
$$	$10 to $15
$$$	$15 to $20
$$$$	$20 to $25
$$$$$	$25 to $30

Prices are for a single entree. Menus and hours of operation frequently change. Call ahead to avoid disappointment.

▼ ▼ ▼ ▼ ▼ ▼ ▼ ▼ ▼ ▼ ▼ ▼ ▼ ▼ ▼ ▼ ▼

Middleton

Louisianne's

7464 Hubbard Avenue
(608) 831-1929

On weekends, the crowds are thick at this snappy subterranean spot just west of Madison. The restaurant feels a little like a wine cave, with its vaulted ceilings and rock walls. But once you're inside, the long copper bar, live music and great Louisianian food will let you know that this restaurant has more to offer than bottles of white and red.

Dinners start with interesting New Orleans-inspired appetizers such as crawfish cheesecake, which is made with ricotta and smoked Gouda cheese, and boiled shrimp with an authentic spicy remoulade sauce. Nightly specials include fresh seafood dishes: sailfish, for example, grilled golden brown and served beneath a melting dollop of lemon butter, and a whole boned chicken breast, char-grilled and topped with sauteed shrimp and Granny Smith apple wedges, then covered with a spicy cranberry-cabernet-orange glaze.

The regular menu lists many Louisianian favorites, such as catfish baked in wine and covered with a sweet Creole mustard sauce, and crawfish etouffee, a spicy dish with lots of chewy little crawfish tails, celery, onions and green peppers. For dessert, don't miss the Cajun cheesecake—a rich, old-fashioned ice-box version piled 3 inches high on a graham-cracker crust.

Open 5 to 9 p.m. Monday; 5 to 10 p.m. Tuesday through Saturday. Closed Sunday. Dinner $ to $$$$. Visa, MasterCard, Discover and American Express accepted. No smoking allowed in the dining area.

▼ ▼ ▼ ▼ ▼ ▼ ▼ ▼ ▼ ▼ ▼ ▼ ▼ ▼ ▼ ▼

EXTRA TIP
Power Gawking

Milwaukee isn't as big as Chicago, but it does get its share of celebrities. So if you're in town and like to look for famous people, you should check out a few of the following spots. Even if you don't see anyone famous, the "ordinary people" watching is good.

Two of the top venues are **Osteria del Mondo** in the Knickerbocker Hotel and **Louise's Trattoria**, both listed elsewhere in this book. Other places to sit and look are:

Mimma's Café, 1307 E. Brady St.; (414) 271-7337. This popular restaurant on Milwaukee's lower East Side is busy every weeknight and jammed on weekends. The restaurant serves a number of interesting Italian dishes and has one of the widest selections of pastas in town. It's also a magnet for local and national glitterati. When film crews come to Milwaukee to make movies, chances are good that both the crews and stars will choose this chic restaurant as the place to unwind.

Elsa's on the Park, 833 N. Jefferson St.; (414) 765-0615. Unlike New Yorkers, who tend to eat late, Milwaukeeans have dinner in the early part of the evening. (Most of the restaurant owners to whom I've spoken say that 7 p.m. is their busiest time.) But there are a few late-night spots. Among them, Elsa's is the best known. Owner Karl Kopp (who also owns the Kopp's custard stands) redecorates the restaurant regularly to keep it fashionable and attract the fashionable crowd. The restaurant is renowned for its great hamburgers, and at night serves an interesting line-up of appetizers, including the best buffalo wings you'll taste this side of New York.

Café at the Pfister, 424 E. Wisconsin Ave.; (414) 273-8222. For out-of-town visitors who stay at the Pfister Hotel, this pleasant hotel coffee shop is often the most convenient place in which to grab a morning meal. That makes it a good spot for checking out famous people who may be in Milwaukee. With its atriumlike feel and well-prepared food, the café is also a nice restaurant in which to rub shoulders with international visitors and local power brokers. Wisconsin Sen. Herb Kohl is a frequent patron.

Milwaukee

Bartolotta's Lake Park Bistro

3133 East Newberry Boulevard
(414) 962-6300

I n the late 1980s and early 1990s, several restaurants in Wisconsin and across the nation began calling themselves bistros. In France, bistros are casual restaurants in which a number of different dishes are served à la carte. Wisconsin restaurateurs used these casual places as rough models. Dishes were à la carte and the atmosphere was casual, but the foods (like three-decker sandwiches and Caesar salads) weren't French.

Joe Bartolotta rebelled against the American bistro movement. So he took over the upper level of the county-owned Lake Park Pavilion (the lower level remains open to the public) and remodeled it into a beautiful restaurant with light Australian cypress floors, attractive hanging lamps and lots of Toulouse-Lautrec reproduction prints. He adopted a genuine French menu, and the restaurant has become one of Milwaukee's gems.

The menu changes regularly, but dishes might include a rich cassoulet (a stew of white beans and preserved duck), foie gras (fresh duck liver) and steak Bearnaise, which comes with *pommes frites*—authentic French fries. There also are patés, terrine and salmon rillettes, which have been slowly cooked to a spreadable consistency and are served with thick slices of toasted French bread. A few pastas and an occasional risotto are on the menu, as well: Bartolotta's Italian restaurant in Wauwatosa (also described in this book) had developed so loyal a following that patrons demanded a few Italian touches.

Part of the restaurant's charm is its location. Lake Park was laid out by the well-known landscape architect Frederick Law Olmsted, who also designed Central Park in New York City. It contains wonderful walking paths and a small golf course, and you can try your hand at lawn bowling in front of the bistro.

Open 11:30 a.m. to 2 p.m. Monday through Friday; 5:30 to 9 p.m. Monday through Thursday; 5:30 to 10 p.m. Friday; 5 to 10 p.m. Saturday; 5 to 8:30 p.m. Sunday. Sunday brunch served 10:30 a.m. to 2 p.m. Lunch $ to $$; dinner $$ to $$$$; brunch $$$. No smoking allowed. All major credit cards accepted.

▼ ▼ ▼ ▼ ▼ ▼ ▼ ▼ ▼ ▼ ▼ ▼ ▼ ▼ ▼ ▼ ▼

Milwaukee
The Boulevard Inn
925 East Wells Street
(414) 765-1166

For years, this elegant establishment was a fixture on Milwaukee's West Side. The restaurant, which has been owned by the Strothmann family for two generations, took its name from Sherman Boulevard, which passed its door. But when a formal room in Milwaukee's elegant Cudahy Towers became available, the Strothmanns took it. Today, the Boulevard Inn overlooks Lake Michigan. And even though it's now on Wells Street, the restaurant hasn't changed its name.

In part, the inn's popularity comes from its atmosphere, which is formal but not stuffy. A pianist performs a mix of popular music and show tunes nightly on a grand piano, and the servers make you feel welcome, not intimidated.

The menu includes old Milwaukee favorites such as veal Oscar and sauerbraten (a German stew), along with an impressive line-up of fresh fish, often grilled and served with flavored butter sauces. Chicken is done differently every day. A breast might be sauteed and served with broccoli and melted cheese, or covered with a rich wine sauce.

Over the years, the Boulevard Inn has maintained a long and well-deserved reputation for the best made-on-the-spot Caesar salad in town. Watching a staff member conduct the ritual—beginning with a lightly cooked egg in the bottom of a large wooden bowl and ending with croutons and shredded cheese—is quite a show. At lunch, the addition of plump freshly cooked shrimp can make those Caesars a delightful entree. Desserts are all homemade and range from rich cheesecake to cream puffs filled with a subtle strawberry cream.

Open 11:30 a.m. to 9 p.m. Monday through Thursday; 11:30 a.m. to 10 p.m. Friday and Saturday; Sunday brunch 10:30 a.m. to 2 p.m. and dinner 11:30 a.m. to 8:30 p.m. Lunch $ to $$; dinner $$$ to $$$$$; brunch $$. All major credit cards accepted. No smoking allowed.

▼ ▼ ▼ ▼ ▼ ▼ ▼ ▼ ▼ ▼ ▼ ▼ ▼ ▼ ▼ ▼ ▼

Milwaukee

Eagan's
1030 North Water Street
(414) 271-6900

I f a visit to Milwaukee includes taking in a performance at one of the downtown theaters, this restaurant may be just right for a before- or after-show meal. Since its opening in the early 1990s, Eagan's has been catering to well-dressed crowds, many of whom are heading for the Marcus Center for the Performing Arts across the street.

Eagan's puts special emphasis on speedy service. An extensive cold seafood bar, serving fresh oysters, clams, crab legs and shrimp, stands beside another long bar offering premium wines by the glass. There's plenty of standing room for people on a brief stop. In addition, a single streamlined menu is used all day long. There's a large selection of hot and cold appetizers (including sushi), warm and cold salads (some of which are topped with meat and fish), sandwiches, burgers, pizzas, entrees and elaborate desserts, the latter being especially popular with the after-show crowd.

Among the restaurant's best dishes are its pizzas, garlic roast chicken and a braised beer steak, which is a fancy name for pot roast braised to tenderness in a slightly sweet tomato-wine gravy. And Eagan's pan-roasted oyster stew can compete with the best New England version of the dish.

The restaurant's 100-seat dining room features large reproductions of French impressionist theater scenes flanked by mirrors and elaborate woodwork above attractively tiled floors.

Open 11 a.m. to 11 p.m. Sunday through Thursday; 11 a.m. to 1 a.m. Friday and Saturday. Lunch and dinner $ to $$$. All major credit cards accepted. No smoking allowed.

Price Key	
$	Under $10
$$	$10 to $15
$$$	$15 to $20
$$$$	$20 to $25
$$$$$	$25 to $30

Prices are for a single entree. Menus and hours of operation frequently change. Call ahead to avoid disappointment.

The English Room
424 East Wisconsin Avenue
(414) 273-8222

Ask any Milwaukeean for a list of the city's classiest restaurants, and this restaurant, located on the lower level of the Pfister Hotel, will most likely be on it. For the past three decades, the English Room has been a prime destination for romantic dinners, important family celebrations and business entertaining.

Everything about this restaurant, from its formal entrance (lined with awards that the restaurant has garnered) to its tuxedoed staff, exudes elegance. In the evening, live music may be provided by a harpist or a classical guitarist, with the sound level appropriate for quiet listening and soft conversation.

Once known for traditional French food, the restaurant's menu has changed over the past few years to include a few lighter dishes. The list of appetizers includes such standards as crab cakes, smoked salmon and an occasional terrine. At dinner, there's an excellent selection of fresh fish and a game entree or two: pan-roasted rabbit, for example, venison chops or quail with figs.

Luncheon offerings include light, trendy dishes from a number of different cuisines, such as rotisserie chicken and stir-fried noodles with a spicy Oriental sauce. Desserts are usually eye-catching and often feature fresh berries atop a delicate custard tart or covered with a luscious Italian sabayon sauce.

Open 11:30 a.m. to 2 p.m. Monday through Friday; 5:30 to 10 p.m. Monday through Friday; 5:30 to 11 p.m. Saturday; 5 to 10 p.m. Sunday. Lunch $ to $$; dinner $$$ to $$$$$. All major credit cards accepted. Small smoking section.

Milwaukee

Grenadier's
747 North Broadway Street
(414) 276-0747

Any short list of Wisconsin's greatest restaurants has to include this highly acclaimed Milwaukee establishment owned by chef Knut Apitz. Apitz was born in Berlin and trained as a chef in Germany. He worked in Switzerland, Holland and Great Britain before coming to the United States in the 1960s. And from the moment he opened Grenadier's in 1975, the restaurant has been known for uncompromising quality and an international menu.

Meals start with two signature dishes: *gaufrettes*—small criss-cross potatoes fried to a crisp and served warm—and pumpernickel bread, also served warm from the oven. But those two dishes are only previews of what's in store.

Apitz works hard to present a balance of old and new on his menu; on a given night, diners can choose between classics, like Tournedoes Rossini, and trendier dishes, such as blue corn crepes with goat cheese. The restaurant's approach to fresh fish is one of the best you'll find anywhere: At the start of a meal, a waiter rolls a portable case of fresh fish on ice to your table and invites you to chose the kind of fish you'd like as well as a method of preparation.

As a boy, Apitz's mother took him to Chinese restaurants, and later in life he worked aboard a cruise ship in the Pacific. So he has a knack for putting an Oriental twist on dishes. Pick the sand dabs (a small, delicate species of sole) and ask for them to be dipped in an egg wash and simply sauteed, and Apitz is likely to brighten the dish with Oriental plum sauce on the side.

Another thing that distinguishes Apitz is his willingness to prepare special orders for his customers. Want sole Veronique? If Apitz has the white grapes, you're in business. This is one place where you don't have to be afraid to ask for something that you don't see on the menu.

In 1996, Chef Charles Weber, formerly of the Park Avenue Café in Chicago, joined the staff. In the coming years, Grenadier's regulars will look to him to keep up the restaurant's tradition of culinary excellence.

Open 11:30 a.m. to 2:30 p.m. Monday through Friday; 5 to 10 p.m. Monday through Saturday. Closed Sunday. Lunch $ to $$; dinner $$ to $$$$$. All major credit cards accepted. Smoking and nonsmoking sections available.

▼ ▼ ▼ ▼ ▼ ▼ ▼ ▼ ▼ ▼ ▼ ▼ ▼ ▼ ▼ ▼ ▼

Milwaukee

Harold's

4747 South Howell Avenue
(414) 481-8000

You've got this problem. For you, going out to dinner is an adventure. You want something new and exciting. Something trendy. The folks who are going with you, however, are not as daring. They want steak. Or lobster.

Look no farther than this elegant restaurant just across the street from Milwaukee's Mitchell International Airport. For years, chef Axel Dietrich has been maintaining a menu that offers all the standard American staples along with more exotic dishes. Depending on when you visit, specials might be French or Mediterranean. And everything from appetizers to desserts shows exceptional culinary creativity.

Rack of lamb almost always appears on the menu and is delicious. Other entrees might be fresh Dover sole amandine, sand dabs (small, delicate filets of Pacific sole) served in a light tomato sauce with fresh herbs, or veal scallops covered with a delicate chanterelle mushroom sauce.

Among the things I like best about Harold's are the crunchy croissants that break apart beautifully between your teeth. Those and the restaurant's elegant desserts are enough to keep me coming back. In addition to great food, Harold's offers diners the perfect setting for a memorable meal. Lighting is subdued and service is excellent.

Open 11:30 a.m. to 2 p.m. Monday through Friday; 5:30 to 10 p.m. Monday through Thursday; 5:30 to 10:30 p.m. Friday and Saturday; 5 to 9 p.m. Sunday, Labor Day through Memorial Day only. Lunch $; dinner $$$ to $$$$$. All major credit cards accepted. Smoking and nonsmoking sections available.

▼ ▼ ▼ ▼ ▼ ▼ ▼ ▼ ▼ ▼ ▼ ▼ ▼ ▼ ▼ ▼ ▼

Milwaukee

Izumi's

2178 North Prospect Avenue
(414) 271-5278

In the 1980s, Milwaukee, like many other cities in America, saw the arrival of sushi. While the thought of eating raw fish on molded rice cakes seemed especially strange in a town known for its sausage and meat stews, these Japanese delights attracted enough of a following to make a couple restaurants more than a fad. One of them is Izumi's, which serves sushi, along with other Japanese dishes, on the city's lower East Side.

Like most Japanese restaurants, Izumi's has a traditional sushi bar that's separate from the cooking area (Japanese chefs believe that cooking odors can ruin the flavor of fresh fish). There's a long list of sushi (served on molded vinegared rice), sashimi (sliced raw fish) and maki (rolled sushi). All are presented in the traditional fashion with preserved ginger to clear the palate and hot green wasabi horseradish to spice things up.

But that's not all. Izumi's also excels at lightly battered, deep-fried tempura; sweet, soy-glazed teriyaki; and katsu, which are breaded pork or chicken cutlets served with a thick, sweet fruit-based sauce. One of the restaurant's most interesting dishes is *shabu-shabu*, the Japanese equivalent of a boiled dinner. To serve it, a waiter or waitress puts a portable butane burner on the table, lights it and swings a heavy iron pot of clear, hot broth onto it. Then comes a platter of paper-thin beef and carrot rounds, fresh pea pods, scallions, mushrooms, tofu, Napa cabbage and udon—thick wheat noodles. You cook everything in the boiling broth, remove the ingredients with chopsticks when they're done, and then dip them in a spicy red sauce made of vinegar, pureed daikon radish, scallions and lemon juice. *Shabu-shabu*, according to Japanese tradition, is the sound that a slice of raw beef makes when it's swirled in hot broth.

If you have any room for dessert, try the green-tea ice cream.

Open 11:30 a.m. to 2:30 p.m. and 5 to 10 p.m. Monday through Thursday; 11:30 a.m. to 2:30 p.m. and 5 to 10:30 p.m. Friday; 5 to 10:30 p.m. Saturday; 4 to 9 p.m. Sunday. Lunch $ to $$; dinner $ to $$$. All major credit cards accepted. Smoking is permitted.

▼ ▼ ▼ ▼ ▼ ▼ ▼ ▼ ▼ ▼ ▼ ▼ ▼ ▼ ▼ ▼

Milwaukee
John Ernst Restaurant
600 East Ogden Avenue
(414) 273-1878

With more than a hundred years of history behind it, this well-known German restaurant claims to be the oldest restaurant in Milwaukee. To date, no contenders have emerged to dispute that claim. Located just north of downtown Milwaukee (it's an easy walk from any of the downtown hotels), the restaurant stands out as a little German island in the midst of a fast-changing urban environment.

Inside, the John Ernst Restaurant looks like it was transported from Bavaria: German beer steins are lined behind the bar, German flags hang from the ceiling, and there's German music on many nights. There's even a sketch of German comedian Paul Hoerbiger frescoed into the plaster on the north wall. And if you want to try German food, this is one of the best places in town.

Schnitzel, the German word for a meat cutlet that's breaded and sauteed, is especially good at John Ernst. The most familiar version of the dish, Wiener schnitzel, is a celebration of simplicity: tender slices of veal breaded in crumbs and then sauteed to a beautiful golden brown. (If you'd like a little more flavor, squeeze lemon over the meat.) Beef rouladen—a tender piece of beef wrapped around a filling of bacon and pickles—is another specialty. The meat is braised and then served in a light gravy with a German potato dumpling on the side. Small German noodles, called spaetzel, are featured with many dishes, as is German sweet-sour red cabbage.

In case you're not in the mood for a heavy German meal, John Ernst has developed an extensive non-German menu. Steaks are top quality, and fresh fish entrees change daily. If yours is a larger party, you might ask for one of the small private dining rooms on the building's west wall: They're very popular for business lunches and family gatherings.

Open 11:45 a.m. to 10:30 p.m. Tuesday through Saturday; 11 a.m. to 10 p.m. Sunday. Closed Monday. Lunch $ to $$; dinner $$ to $$$$$. All major credit cards accepted. Smoking (including cigars) and nonsmoking sections available.

99

▼ ▼ ▼ ▼ ▼ ▼ ▼ ▼ ▼ ▼ ▼ ▼ ▼ ▼ ▼ ▼ ▼

Milwaukee

Karl Ratzsch's Old World Restaurant
320 East Mason Street
(414) 276-2720

S it down in this restaurant, one of the most famous German places in Milwaukee, notice the antlers on the chandeliers, and let your imagination run free. You might think you were in a German hunting lodge. In actuality, the building that is now the restaurant housed a bank until the Depression put it out of business. (The bank's safe, which was too big and heavy to move, is still in the restaurant's basement.)

While the menu at Ratzsch's these days lists fresh fish, many of the restaurant's fans come for the traditional food it's been serving for almost a century. Schnitzels are breaded and delicately sauteed, rouladen are carefully wrapped and braised, and goose, with its delicious dark gravy, is slowly steam-roasted to render it flavorful and tender. And the sauerbraten, with its delightful, sweet note, is the best you'll find anywhere.

All the appropriate side dishes are served. There are crisp, deep-green spinach salads with hot bacon dressing, liver dumpling soup, homemade potato dumplings and spaetzel (German noodles), red cabbage and sauerkraut, and fresh rye rolls studded with salt crystals. All can be accompanied by a number of good German beers. And if there's any room left, schaum mocha and chocolate tortes are featured on the dessert menu. Everything is served in a warm, typically German atmosphere with piano music nightly. Waitresses wear traditional German dresses.

Open 4 to 9:30 p.m. Monday through Friday; 4 to 10:30 p.m. Saturday; 4 to 9 p.m. Sunday. Dinner $$ to $$$$. All major credit cards accepted. No smoking allowed.

▼ ▼ ▼ ▼ ▼ ▼ ▼ ▼ ▼ ▼ ▼ ▼ ▼ ▼ ▼ ▼ ▼

Milwaukee

Louise's Trattoria
801 North Jefferson Street
(414) 273-4224

Don't be surprised if sitting in this popular downtown restaurant feels a little like eating out in Los Angeles. The restaurant's sleek Italian decor (ultra-modern hanging lamps and metallic accents) looks like a movie set. And that's no accident. The restaurant belongs to a successful California chain with outlets in Beverly Hills, Redondo Beach and Santa Monica. Milwaukee was its first location outside California. (Jon Chait, the brother of owner Bill Chait, lives in the area and has an interest in the restaurant.)

Decor aside, Louise's food is the element that keeps its customers lined up at the bar and waiting for tables. The restaurant's pizzas, pastas, salads and other Italian dishes are both reasonably priced and flavorful. Some of the pasta entrees, such as tagliatelle with Bologneses sauce, are standouts. Tagliatelle are thin, flat noodles, about a third as wide as fettuccine; Bolognese is a tomato sauce with ground meat. The combination works wonderfully. Another tasty dish is rigatoni and grilled vegetables—pasta with zucchini, summer squash and broccoli, all drizzled with olive oil and wood-roasted. The smoky flavor of the vegetables permeates the dish. Chicken ravioli and penne rigate (thin, ribbed tubes of pasta) in pesto sauce with asparagus, mushrooms and sun-dried tomatoes are also worth sampling.

Louise's also offers crisp made-to-order pizzas with an assortment of California-style toppings, great minestrone soup and chopped salads, all of which are reasonably priced.

Open 11 a.m. to 11 p.m. Sunday through Thursday; 11 a.m. to midnight Friday and Saturday. Lunch and dinner $ to $$$. All major credit cards accepted. Smoking and nonsmoking sections available.

Price Key
$ Under $10
$$ $10 to $15
$$$ $15 to $20
$$$$ $20 to $25
$$$$$ $25 to $30
Prices are for a single entree. Menus and hours of operation frequently change. Call ahead to avoid disappointment.

▼ ▼ ▼ ▼ ▼ ▼ ▼ ▼ ▼ ▼ ▼ ▼ ▼ ▼ ▼ ▼ ▼ ▼ ▼ ▼

EXTRA TIP

Chili for
Chilly Days

Milwaukee has other food traditions besides German. One of them is distinctly American. You'll find it at **Real Chili**, a restaurant that's been serving up bowls and bowls of spicy ground beef with beans and spaghetti since 1931.

The restaurant has two locations, both of which are unpretentious. The East Town Real Chili, at 419 E. Wells St. (414-271-4042) is the more upscale of the two, with a few tables in addition to a counter. The West Side Real Chili at 1625 W. Wells St. (414-342-6955) is most popular with students from Marquette University. All of the seats here are at a counter.

On cold days in fall, winter and spring (warm weather doesn't arrive in Milwaukee until after Memorial Day), Real Chili serves hundreds of bowls of chili. At the East Side location, it's fashionable to either toss your tie over your shoulder or tuck it inside your shirt. And don't be surprised if the person sitting next to you is a bank official or a federal judge; professionals stop in for their chili fixes at regular intervals.

The chili comes in three temperatures—mild, medium and hot. The mainstay is ladled over spaghetti and beans and is called a Marquette Special. From there, you can add toppings, such as cheese, onions and sour cream. The chili dogs are real winners. And if you're one of those fire-breathers who isn't satisfied by what comes out of the kitchen, there's ground chile and pepper-laced vinegar available on the counter to add to your meal. Use them with care.

▼ ▼ ▼ ▼ ▼ ▼ ▼ ▼ ▼ ▼ ▼ ▼ ▼ ▼ ▼ ▼

Milwaukee

Mike and Anna's

2000 South 8th Street
(414) 643-0072

I f you weren't looking for it, you could easily pass the corner of South 8th and West Rogers streets and pay no attention to the small stone-fronted building on the southeast corner. From the outside, Mike and Anna's restaurant looks like an average bar in an average working-class neighborhood.

Things become more obvious at dinner time, when the Cadillacs, Lexuses and even an occasional Excalibur are parked outside. But to really appreciate this marvelous little restaurant, you have to follow the well-heeled drivers of those fancy cars inside.

Sit down at one of the tables, notice the stylish decor, have the specials of the day recited to you, and then take your first bite of smoked salmon or your first spoonful of mango or pepper cream soup. Then you will understand how interesting a meal awaits you.

The restaurant's surreal interior includes a long high window from which a small galaxy of tiny lights glitters like the night sky. The dining room's north wall is decorated with long, spearlike shafts, each tipped with ornate, hand-blown bulbs that glow like gas flames from the shiny shafts. The focal point of the room is a large plastic board on which the appetizers, entrees and desserts of the night are listed.

For appetizers, you might try sweet surf clams or veal sweetbreads sauteed and covered with a sweet honey-veal glaze. For entrees, there are always several fresh fish as well as poultry dishes, such as grilled breast of duck sliced into medallions, then fanned out atop a lively sauce of tart Door County cherries. Meat entrees include veal, lamb and tornedoes of beef, made even more luscious by slivers of Stilton cheese and a sauce of brandy, red wine and shallots.

Desserts are as creative as the entrees. One of the house specialties is a three-tiered black and white cake—a rich layer of chocolate cake sandwiched between two light vanilla layers. Coffee-flavored butter cream binds the creation together.

Open 5:30 to 9 p.m. Tuesday through Thursday and Sunday; 5:30 to 10 p.m. Friday and Saturday. Closed Monday and major holidays. Dinner $$$ to $$$$$. MasterCard, Visa and American Express accepted. No smoking allowed.

▼ ▼ ▼ ▼ ▼ ▼ ▼ ▼ ▼ ▼ ▼ ▼ ▼ ▼ ▼ ▼

Milwaukee

Osteria del Mondo

1028 East Juneau Avenue
(414) 291-3770

During the last few years, a number of new Italian restaurants have opened in Milwaukee. The Osteria del Mondo, located in the Knickerbocker Hotel, is clearly one of the best. The talented man behind the restaurant is chef and owner Mark Bianchini, a graduate of the Culinary Institute of America who worked in restaurants in New York and Italy before moving to Milwaukee.

In Italy, an "osteria" is a tavern or inn where folks congregate to socialize as well as to eat. So while Milwaukee's business set may show up for dinner here in suits, other patrons dress more casually. The restaurant's dining room has an understated elegance, with bleached hardwood floors and white tablecloths.

Bianchini's approach to Italian food varies from complex dishes like chicken breast stuffed with polenta (a corn dish popular in northern Italy) and drizzled with a rich, dark chicken glaze, to simpler ones, such as pork chops seasoned with fresh rosemary and roasted with potatoes and onions. Bianchini also prepares fresh fish in light garlic broths that treat diners to delightful scents before they take their first bite.

Simple appetizers like fried calamari and zucchini are so expertly done that you might feel as if you're tasting the dishes for the first time. Bianchini's bruschetta is the best in town. The grilled slices of oiled and garlicked Italian bread are topped with fresh tomato, melted mozzarella and slices of top-quality prosciutto to create delicious open-faced sandwiches. The osteria's pastas and salads all have distinctively Italian flavors, and some of the restaurant's desserts are flown in fresh from Italy.

Open 11:30 a.m. to 2:30 p.m. Monday through Friday; 5 to 10:30 p.m. Monday through Thursday; 5 to 11 p.m. Friday and Saturday; 5 to 9 p.m. Sunday; Sunday brunch served 10 a.m. to 2 p.m. Lunch $ to $$; dinner $$ to $$$; brunch $$$. MasterCard, Visa, Diner's Club and American Express accepted. No smoking allowed.

▼ ▼ ▼ ▼ ▼ ▼ ▼ ▼ ▼ ▼ ▼ ▼ ▼ ▼ ▼ ▼

Milwaukee

Sanford

1547 North Jackson Street
(414) 276-9608

Since its opening in December 1989, this exquisite restaurant has attracted quite a bit of national attention. In its first year of operation, John F.
Mariani, restaurant critic for *Esquire*, named it one of the 10 best new
restaurants in America. In 1996, owner Sandy D'Amato received a James Beard
Award as best chef in the Midwest. He has also been featured in *Bon Appetit*
magazine and on national television.

Despite all that acclaim, D'Amato hasn't forgotten his roots: The chic restaurant that he owns with his wife, Angie, was his father's grocery store. (The
grocery store's scale is on display in the dining room.) Sandy and his family
once lived in the apartment upstairs.

What garners acclaim is D'Amato's knack for combining dishes and flavors
in new and exciting ways. When chefs began preparing their fresh fish in flavorful broths, D'Amato offered his diners seared Alaskan halibut in a mushroom crust with an intensely flavored mushroom broth. When squab came into
vogue, D'Amato roasted the birds with a maple glaze and served them with foie
gras on his own bacon oatcakes with oven-dried plum salad on the side.

Some dishes appear on the menu with the seasons. D'Amato salutes each
spring with a celebratory saute of wild mushrooms, fiddleheads, ramps (wild
onions) and Yukon Gold potatoes. Other dishes are always available, like D'A-
mato's Provencale fish soup with *rouille* (a spicy sauce made of bread crumbs
and olive oil) and his famous pear and Roquefort cheese tart, which he served
to Julia Child.

In recent years, Sanford has also become a place in which to enjoy ethnic
cuisine. D'Amato picks a different country each month and, Monday through
Thursday, serves an elaborate five-course, fixed-price dinner along with the
usual menu. That means that visiting the restaurant on a weeknight can present you with a pleasant quandary: You can travel to an exotic land by ordering the ethnic dinner, or stay at home and enjoy Sandy D'Amato's nightly
flights of culinary fancy, choosing a dish that's listed on the regular menu.

*Open 5:30 to 9 p.m. Monday through Thursday; 5:30 to 10 p.m. Friday and
Saturday. Closed Sunday and all major holidays. Dinner $$$$ to $$$$$$.
MasterCard, Visa, American Express, Diner's Club and Discover accepted. No
smoking allowed.*

▼ ▼ ▼ ▼ ▼ ▼ ▼ ▼ ▼ ▼ ▼ ▼ ▼ ▼ ▼ ▼ ▼ ▼

Mukwonago

Heaven City
S91-W27850 County ES
(414) 363-5191

The building that houses this restaurant has been a local landmark for three-quarters of a century. Located just north of Mukwonago, the main building was originally a sprawling, Spanish-style home built in the 1920s by Milwaukee tobacco dealer George Schuster. In 1932 it was taken over by fiery preacher A.J. Moore, who established a religious commune on the grounds and supported it with a school and hotel. The commune developed a questionable reputation because of Moore's penchant for enrolling young female disciples whom he referred to as "angels," and who provided companionship to some of Moore's favored male guests at the hotel. Moore, whose picture hangs in the bar and after whom owner and chef Scott McGlinchey named the house hamburger, died in 1961.

These days, the delightful art deco building has become a showcase for McGlinchey's culinary creations. McGlinchey is a master at showcasing the foods of Wisconsin in new and interesting ways, from his Barron County wood-roasted chicken to his delicate turnovers filled with trout from farms in the nearby Kettle Moraine area. Entrees like garlic-crusted filet mignon, duck with Door County cherry sauce or wood-roasted salmon regularly appear on the menu, along with other interesting dishes, such as Oriental-style steamed dumplings filled with bratwurst, and Italian linguine with smoked pheasant sauce. Each fall, McGlinchey does a one-week wild-game menu.

Desserts are just as creative. McGlinchey's custard-apple tart is a favorite and his souffles are light and delicious. Consider ordering one when you order your entree so it will be done when you are ready to eat it.

Open 11:30 a.m. to 2 p.m. Monday through Friday; 5:30 to 9:30 p.m. Monday through Saturday; 5 to 9 p.m. Sunday. Lunch $; dinner $$ to $$$$. All major credit cards accepted. No smoking allowed.

Nashotah
Red Circle Inn
N44-W33013 Watertown Plank Road
(414) 367-4883

Fine food has been served at this Waukesha County restaurant for the better part of a century and a half, give or take a few years. The story of the restaurant begins in 1847 when a stagecoach stop was constructed on the road from Milwaukee to Watertown. That building was destroyed by fire in 1917. It was rebuilt and family operated until 1975, when it was bought by the Provimi Veal Co. Under that company's ownership, the Red Circle Inn became widely renowned for wonderful food and elegant service.

The restaurant closed for a few years, reopened in 1991 and has been on the comeback trail ever since. These days it's owned by Norm Ecksteadt and Nico Derni, who trained in France. The two men also own the Elm Grove Inn (also described in this book). They have made the Red Circle better than ever, with a country inn menu that features classically made French patés, great veal, lamb and fish.

The menu changes regularly, but culinary creativity is a constant. Instead of the standard French onion soup, the inn has offered three-onion soup au gratin flavored with port wine and covered with browned and bubbling Swiss cheese. One rendition of creamy shrimp bisque has a little bourbon added. For entrees, the menu might list Barbarie duck breast with New Orleans sausage, an elegant-looking dish that fans slices of grilled duck breast around a thick slice of grilled duck sausage, with a mound of wild rice and a rich duck sauce on the side. Or there might be fresh salmon, poached with dill, then served atop a stone-ground mustard sauce with buttered pasta on the side. One of the most impressive dishes is a ballotine of chicken—chicken completely boned, then rolled around a filling of finely chopped chicken and gently poached in broth. Served in slices, it's both beautiful and delicious.

Desserts are likely to be just as dramatic. Double chocolate mousse mounds light, creamy milk-chocolate mousse atop a darker rendition of the dish and surrounds both with delicate custard sauce. And a Napoleon of fresh berries puts fresh raspberries and strawberries atop vanilla custard on a light puff-pastry crust.

Open 5 to 9:30 p.m. Tuesday through Saturday. Closed Sunday and Monday. Dinner $$$ to $$$$. MasterCard, Visa, Discover and American Express accepted. Smoking and nonsmoking sections available.

▼ ▼ ▼ ▼ ▼ ▼ ▼ ▼ ▼ ▼ ▼ ▼ ▼ ▼ ▼ ▼ ▼ ▼

EXTRA TIP

Swiss Scene

Wisconsin has always honored its ethnic traditions. One place in which they run strong is New Glarus, about 30 miles southwest of Madison. In the 1800s, the town was settled by a group of immigrants from the canton of Glarus in Switzerland.

Today, New Glarus is a delight. One bakery specializes in Swiss pastries, the meat market makes and sells Swiss-style sausage, and several stores offer Swiss chocolate. And at the **New Glarus Hotel**, 100 6th Ave. (608-527-5244), Swiss meals are still served. Cheese and beef fondues are available, along with *roesti*, a side dish of potatoes and cheese, which accompanies many of the restaurant's entrees. The hotel serves buffet-style on Friday nights and on Sundays for brunch. The Sunday spread is extensive, with more than 20 items.

If you're looking for more European flavor, try **Deininger's**, 119 5th Ave. (608-527-2012). The restaurant is housed in one of New Glarus' old mansions. Its owner and chef, Roland Deininger, was born in Alsace and apprenticed there, and has worked in Paris and in Switzerland. So don't be surprised if French beef stew is listed between German-style sauerbraten and Hungarian-style veal steak with paprika. One of Deininger's specialties is *Konigsberg Klopse*, a hearty stew of beef and veal with capers.

▼   ▼   ▼   ▼   ▼   ▼   ▼   ▼   ▼   ▼   ▼   ▼   ▼   ▼   ▼   ▼

New Berlin

Steven Wade's Café
17001 West Greenfield Avenue
(414) 784-0774

Anyone who visits this impressive restaurant in Milwaukee's western suburbs and revels in its creative food owes some gratitude to the Hyatt Regency. The Hyatt brought Steven Wade Klindt to Milwaukee in 1984. After two years of working as the downtown hotel restaurant's executive chef, Klindt and his wife, Judy, decided they wanted a place of their own.

They bought an old building that had housed a paint store, went to work remodeling it and opened it in 1986 as Steven Wade's Café. In those days, the restaurant had only 40 seats, and Klindt penned the day's specials onto a small erasable menu board in the dining room. From delicate, homemade ravioli stuffed with choice crab to hearty steaks seared with peppers and finished with jalapeno vodka, Klindt's creative menu attracted such waves of devotees that he quickly expanded his restaurant to seat 55.

Those extra 15 seats give more diners the opportunity to try Klindt's dishes. These days, the menus are written out and have two distinct sides. On the left, Klindt lists popular entrees that are available night after night. The other side lists delights of the day.

For appetizers, Klindt might offer Maryland crab cakes and herb ravioli atop a cool sauce made of apricots, habanero chilies and freshly ground vanilla, or pecan-crusted sea scallops served with herbed mayonnaise. In the entree department, there might be Chilean sea bass with crayfish risotto on a coriander-ginger-lime butter, or zucchini pancakes with seared calico scallops, roasted-tomato vinaigrette and crispy fried parsnips. Duck, veal and beef are almost always on the menu and prepared in equally creative fashion. Desserts might range from chocolate mousse wrapped in a delicious light chocolate cake to fresh blackberry crisp, served warm with homemade ice cream melting on its crust.

Open 11:30 a.m. to 2 p.m. Tuesday through Friday; 5:30 to 10 p.m. Monday through Saturday. Closed Sunday. Lunch $ to $$; dinner $$$ to $$$$. All major credit cards accepted. No smoking allowed.

▼ ▼ ▼ ▼ ▼ ▼ ▼ ▼ ▼ ▼ ▼ ▼ ▼ ▼ ▼ ▼

Port Washington
Buchel's Colonial House
1000 South Spring Street
(414) 375-1180

This well-established restaurant on Port Washington's southwest side carries on a tradition that spans three generations. Walter Buchel, who came to America from Liechtenstein in 1947, opened the restaurant in 1976. Much of Walter's training came from his father, Joseph, who had worked in hotels throughout Europe and once served as chef to the Prince of Liechtenstein. In 1988, Walter sold the restaurant to his son, who is also named Joseph.

While the restaurant's decor is, as its name indicates, Early American, with Windsor chairs, fine-print wallpaper and a lot of country accents, its menu has a strong European influence. There's the Buchel version of the traditional French steak au poivre, which is studded with freshly cracked peppercorns, and a version of veal saltimbocca that's filled with ham, mushrooms, spinach and mozzarella cheese. But not all the Colonial House's entrees are European: The restaurant also serves steaks and barbecued ribs.

Meals begin with one of the most interesting appetizer platters in the state: a lazy Susan loaded with an ever-changing array of spreads, pickles and special appetizers, such as miniature meatballs and marinated turkey chunks. Chocoholics will appreciate Colonial House desserts: white chocolate mousse with raspberry sauce, for example, and a rich dark-chocolate mousse cake.

Open 5 to 10 p.m. Tuesday through Saturday. Closed Sunday and Monday. Dinner $$ to $$$$. Visa and MasterCard accepted. Smoking and nonsmoking sections available.

▼ ▼ ▼ ▼ ▼ ▼ ▼ ▼ ▼ ▼ ▼ ▼ ▼ ▼ ▼ ▼

Port Washington

The Port Hotel
101 East Main Street
(414) 284-6195

In tourist season, Port Washington's renovated lakefront draws flocks of tourists, who often choose to dine at the lakefront restaurants that offer a view of the water. Many of Port Washington's residents, on the other hand, prefer to have dinner a few blocks west, at the Port Hotel.

Like many turn-of-the-century hotels in Wisconsin, the Port Hotel no longer accommodates overnight guests. Its main business is its restaurant, which is known throughout the area for excellent prime rib, steaks and delicious fried walleye and lake perch.

The Port Hotel's dining rooms have a traditional feeling. The front room, with ornate hanging lamps, is the most Victorian of the three; a middle room looks like an English hunt club. The restaurant's busiest area seems to be its bar, where a steady stream of patrons is usually waiting for tables.

Dinners at the Port Hotel begin with a relish tray laden with radishes, carrot and celery sticks, black olives and pickles, marinated carrot salad, cottage cheese and homemade liver paté. Served with fresh bread, it makes a good start to a meal. In addition to great beef, the restaurant offers daily specials, such as grilled or blackened fish and an occasional German dish. Fried perch is dipped in crumbs and delivered crisp and golden from the fryer. One of the best parts of dinner at the Port Hotel is dessert. Cheesecake and tarts are offered daily, but many people prefer the signature dessert, banana cream pie.

Open 11 a.m. to 2 p.m. Monday through Friday; 5 to 10 p.m. Monday through Thursday; 5 to 11 p.m. Friday and Saturday; 10 a.m. to 2 p.m. and 3 to 9 p.m. Sunday. Lunch $; dinner $ to $$$. All major credit cards accepted. No smoking allowed on weekends and holidays; smoking section available Monday through Thursday.

Price Key	
$	Under $10
$$	$10 to $15
$$$	$15 to $20
$$$$	$20 to $25
$$$$$	$25 to $30

Prices are for a single entree. Menus and hours of operation frequently change. Call ahead to avoid disappointment.

▼ ▼ ▼ ▼ ▼ ▼ ▼ ▼ ▼ ▼ ▼ ▼ ▼ ▼ ▼ ▼

Racine

The Corner House

1521 Washington Avenue
(414) 637-1295

E ven though it's a simple dish, most folks don't make prime rib at home, except for major occasions. You need a large piece of beef, a large oven and the right technique to turn out a perfect piece of prime. For the past 50 years, Corner House owner Al Kopulos has been facing that challenge nightly. Since he opened the Corner House in 1945, he's made his restaurant synonymous with prime rib. Available in three different cuts, the prime rib at the Corner House is everything it should be—flavorful, moist and almost tender enough to cut with a fork.

Of course, that's not all that the Corner House has to offer its guests. The restaurant, which is now run by Al Kopulos' son, George, has a lengthy menu that includes excellent veal and poultry dishes, many of which have an Italian flavor. Roast duck and ribs are also topnotch.

All of the desserts are good, but one stands out. Cherry cheesecake is topped with Kopulos' own brandied cherries. As an alternative, you can taste those cherries on top of a sundae.

The dining room has a formal look, with white tablecloths on the tables, foil wallpaper, large floral displays and a collection of Toulouse-Lautrec reproductions. It's a popular spot for both business types and casually dressed diners.

Open 5 to 9:30 p.m. Monday through Thursday; 5 to 10:15 p.m. Friday and Saturday; 4 to 8:30 p.m. Sunday. Dinner $$ to $$$$$. All major credit cards accepted. Smoking and nonsmoking sections available.

▼ ▼ ▼ ▼ ▼ ▼ ▼ ▼ ▼ ▼ ▼ ▼ ▼ ▼ ▼ ▼ ▼

East Garden Chinese Restaurant

3600 North Oakland Avenue
(414) 962-7460

D rive past the red brick building with the round door at the intersection of Oakland and Menlo avenues, and you might find it hard to believe that it once housed a gas station. That's testimony to the skill of China-born artist Sik Kin Wu, who undertook the transformation in 1983. Since then, the building has housed one of the best Chinese restaurants in southeastern Wisconsin.

East Garden is a casual place with a regular menu so extensive that making a choice is difficult. Regulars diners know that Wu's latest creations—and East Garden's most interesting dishes—are listed on the front pages of the menu. In recent years, these have included chicken, beef and shrimp cooked with fresh strawberries, and tasty stir-fries of meat or shrimp with crisp, fresh asparagus.

Wu's chilled broccoli appetizer sticks (served with carrot chunks), marinated in a sweet and sour rice wine mix, make an excellent first course. Another great way to start dinner is with a simple Chinese soup called Three Delights. It combines shrimp, chicken chunks, slices of reddened barbecued Chinese pork, sliced pea pods, napa cabbage, scallions, water chestnuts and mushrooms in a well-made Chinese stock.

East Garden also has one of the best selections of vegetarian entrees in the Milwaukee area. Spicy fresh string beans, a western Chinese dish, are the yard-long variety often seen in Oriental markets. Cooking them is a two-step process. The beans are first deep-fried in peanut oil. Once cooked and drained, they're stir-fried with spicy preserved Sichuan mustard greens, then covered with a light soy sauce. For nonvegetarians, variations of the dish are available with shrimp, pork or beef. Another wonderful meat entree pairs crispy chicken with walnuts. Sesame beef, chicken or pork are also very good. And the restaurant's luncheon buffet is one of the best in town.

Wu ran into some problems with the federal government and, in 1995, pleaded guilty to tax fraud and was sentenced to 18 months in prison. But so far those problems haven't affected the food or service.

Open 11:30 a.m. to 10 p.m. Monday through Thursday; 11:30 a.m. to 11 p.m. Friday; 3 to 11 p.m. Saturday; 11:30 a.m. to 9:30 p.m. Sunday. Lunch and dinner $ to $$. MasterCard, Visa and American Express accepted. Smoking and non-smoking sections available.

113

▼ ▼ ▼ ▼ ▼ ▼ ▼ ▼ ▼ ▼ ▼ ▼ ▼ ▼ ▼ ▼ ▼

Stone Bank

Sally's Meat N Place
N67 West 33525 County K
(414) 367-1288

In the 1970s and 1980s, Sally's Steak House in the Knickerbocker Hotel routinely made it onto every list of top state restaurants. The restaurant served good food and was a prime spot to see local celebrities. Owned and operated by Sally Papia, it developed a solid reputation for steaks and Italian dishes. Papia prided herself on making the spaghetti sauce and soup fresh each day.

Papia was also one of Milwaukee's more colorful characters. She did time in prison in 1975 for extortion and again in 1991 for making illegal payments to a union so it would not organize her restaurant employees. She lost her popular downtown restaurant in a much-publicized court fight with her daughter, Candy. Other people might have folded under the weight of all those troubles; Sally Papia did not. In 1994, she bought the Meat N Place, a popular Waukesha lake country restaurant. Her fans have been flocking to it ever since.

Part of the attraction is Sally herself, who's been known to wear glitter-edged eyeglasses as she walks through the dining room and to leave the Christmas decorations up until Easter. But most of the restaurant's popularity is due to its well-prepared, reasonably priced food.

Dinners at Sally's start with a relish tray that includes black olives, carrot and celery sticks, pickles and cocktail peppers, and a basket of freshly sliced Italian bread. Then there's Sally's famous chicken pastina soup, which features tiny grains of Italian pasta, chunks of chicken and carrots in a fragrant homemade chicken broth that's tinged with just enough tomato to make it glisten reddish-gold.

Sally's has always served great steaks, and the house filet mignon and a Sicilian-style steak are especially good. Veal Marsala (with sweet Italian wine) and Veal Sarina (with breaded eggplant) are also topnotch. So is pan-fried chicken with mushrooms.

A note of warning: When you go to Sally's, be prepared to wait. Having to drive 30 miles out of town hasn't put off her followers one bit.

Open 4:30 to 9 p.m. Tuesday through Thursday and Sunday; 4:30 to 10 p.m. Friday and Saturday. Closed Monday. Dinner $$ to $$$$. MasterCard and Visa accepted. Smoking and nonsmoking sections available.

WolfenDale's
N63-W23929 Main Street
(414) 246-4601

This delightful restaurant opened in the spring of 1996 and within two months was thronged with diners. What attracted them?

Partly, the building's charm. With its high-beamed ceilings, natural wood floors and lace window treatments, WolfenDale's has an air of simple elegance. Diners dress casually, but white tablecloths, blue napkins and small fresh floral arrangements give the 60-seat restaurant an air of sophistication. Add to that a beautiful huge stone fireplace and you have the right setting for a good meal, especially in the winter months when the roaring fire can chase a chill.

But it takes more than atmosphere to draw a crowd. WolfenDale's strongest lure is its food. The restaurant's menu features steaks, chops and fresh fish, embellished with herb butters and simple sauces. Among the entrees that appear frequently on the menu is Pork Porterhouse, a thick pork chop marinated in olive oil with juniper berries and Tanqueray gin. The combination gives the meat's exterior a lively taste that contrasts nicely with its mild natural flavor. Ribs, fish and chicken are also quite good. Grouper, for example, is grilled and covered with a mild puree of sweet peppers. Chicken Arthur is surprisingly rich—two grilled breasts served atop warm mushroom couscous and covered with a rich brown garlic sauce.

Diners can choose two of seven side dishes. Among them are couscous (a fine pasta that's widely served in northern Africa), angel hair pasta with garlic butter, baked Idaho potatoes and garden salads. Desserts are simple but delicious. Fresh strawberries, for example, are served with a light custard sauce. Even the chocolate mousse is light; it's served chilled in a tall glass.

Open 11:30 a.m. to 2 p.m. Monday through Friday; 5 to 9 p.m. Monday through Thursday; 5 to 10 p.m. Friday and Saturday. Closed Sunday. Lunch $ to $$; dinner $$ to $$$. MasterCard, Visa and American Express accepted. No smoking allowed.

Waukesha

Ching Hwa
1947 East Main Street
(414) 544-1983

A lot of Chinese restaurants in Wisconsin aren't ostentatious places. They're ordinary buildings, occasionally with a characteristically Chinese round doorway. Ching Hwa in Waukesha is a major exception. Located on a hill above busy Highway 18, the restaurant has large pillars and a pagodalike roof. Inside, there's elaborately carved woodwork, ornate Chinese ceiling tiles and lots of Chinese art. And during most of the hours that it's open, the restaurant is filled with customers.

Food is what makes Ching Hwa such a popular place. The restaurant bills itself as a northern Chinese establishment, which means it offers a wide variety of dishes. In the days of Imperial China, chefs from across the country were recruited to work in the emperor's palace in the northern capital city of Beijing. Each brought different skills and ingredients, so the cooking in the capital city (and across northern China) became an elaborate combination of elements from all the other regions of the country.

It's hard to pick which of Ching Hwa's dishes are best, but you might want to start off with an elaborate Chinese soup called *san shan* sizzling rice. The soup is delivered in an ornate tureen that holds hot broth laden with plump shrimp, tender scallops, crunchy pea pods, bamboo shoots and freshly sliced mushrooms. At the last moment, the server spoons in several small rice cakes still hot from the fryer. They explode into steam and give the soup a pleasant textural contrast, like fried croutons in Western soups.

Smoked tea duck is marinated in sweetened soy sauce, then fried to produce a delightfully crispy skin on top of moist meat. Princess chicken is a spicy stir-fry of diced chicken, carrots, water chestnuts, celery, bamboo shoots, green peppers, hot peppers, onions and peanuts in a clear, lightly flavored sauce.

If you're in the mood for something out of the ordinary, try the sea cucumbers, which are also known as sea slugs. They may sound unappetizing, but are very good, served in a rich brown sauce with black mushrooms and pork.

Open 11:30 a.m. to 2 p.m. Monday through Friday; 11:30 a.m. to 2:30 p.m. Sunday; 5 to 10 p.m. Monday through Thursday; 5 to 10:30 p.m. Friday and Saturday; 5 to 9:30 p.m. Sunday. Lunch $; dinner $ to $$$. MasterCard, Visa, American Express and Discover cards accepted.

▾ ▾ ▾ ▾ ▾ ▾ ▾ ▾ ▾ ▾ ▾ ▾ ▾ ▾ ▾ ▾ ▾

Waukesha

Weisgerber Gasthaus Restaurant
2720 North Grandview Boulevard
(414) 544-4460

If you're looking for a place to enjoy German food and atmosphere but don't want to deal with downtown Milwaukee, this restaurant on Waukesha's west side is your best bet. The Gasthaus looks and feels as if it had been moved to Wisconsin directly from Germany. Ceilings, trim, hanging lamps and pictures all have an authentic German look to them. The restaurant's sauerbraten, rouladen and classic German meat platters are also wonderfully authentic. And the Gasthaus is the only spot in the Milwaukee area that serves a classic German salad, in which each ingredient is prepared and presented separately.

Among the entrees, you'll find *kasseler rippchen* (smoked pork chops), sausage platters, and turkey and veal schnitzels. If you're interested in trying more than one German food at a time, you can order a combination platter. All the appropriate side dishes, such as potato dumplings, spaetzel (German egg noodles), red cabbage and sauerkraut taste like they were flown in from Germany. Soups are especially hearty and good. For dessert, don't miss the Gasthaus' rum cake. With coffee, it puts a wonderful finish on a hearty meal.

Open 11:30 a.m. to 2:30 p.m. Monday through Friday; 5 to 10 p.m. Monday through Saturday; 4 to 9 p.m. Sunday. Lunch $ to $$; dinner $$$ to $$$$. MasterCard, Visa and American Express accepted. Smoking and nonsmoking sections available.

▼ ▼ ▼ ▼ ▼ ▼ ▼ ▼ ▼ ▼ ▼ ▼ ▼ ▼ ▼ ▼ ▼

Wauwatosa

Ristorante Bartolotta

7616 West State Street
(414) 771-7910

Walk into this popular Italian restaurant in Milwaukee's western suburbs and you might lose your sense of place for a minute. You know you're in the Village of Wauwatosa. So why does it feel like New York? The answer, simply put, is owner Joe Bartolotta, who with the help of his brother, Paul, a well-known chef at Spiaggia in Chicago, put together the setting and the menu for this classy Italian restaurant. (Bartolotta also operates the Lake Park Bistro, described elsewhere in this book.)

At the heart of Ristorante Bartolotta is a wood-fired oven that's fired up in the morning. At lunch and dinner, it turns out small crispy pizzas and slow-roasted meats, fish and poultry that have the fragrant flavor of wood. These specialties are only part of the restaurant's allure, however. Order the simplest of pastas and you'll be amazed at how good fresh tomatoes, basil and garlic can taste. Other excellent entrees are duck with wide homemade noodles and linguine with fresh clams served in the shell. Even simpler entrees, like chicken, pork and veal chops, roasted with garlic and rosemary, are distinctive.

Ristorante Bartolotta augments those wonderful pastas and entrees with lots of other Italian touches. Thick, chewy country-style bread tastes like it came from an oven in Florence; mozzarella salad features small balls of the Italian cheese made from water buffalo milk. And for dessert, there are Italian ices and ice creams, made on the premises, along with rich tiramisu, a cheesecake flavored with coffee and chocolate.

For years, the Bartolotta family has been in the fireworks business and is well-known for its spectacular displays on Fourth of July and during Milwaukee's annual Festa Italiana. When asked if he's related to the pyrotechnic Bartolottas, Joe says, "Yes. We're all in the entertainment business. Only they do theirs in the sky and I do mine on the tables."

Open 11:30 a.m. to 2 p.m. Monday through Friday; 5:30 to 10 p.m. Monday through Thursday; 5:30 to 10:30 p.m. Friday and Saturday. Closed Sunday and all major holidays. Lunch $ to $$$; dinner $$ to $$$$. All major credit cards accepted. No smoking allowed.

▼ ▼ ▼ ▼ ▼ ▼ ▼ ▼ ▼ ▼ ▼ ▼ ▼ ▼ ▼ ▼ ▼ ▼

Pleasant Valley Inn
9801 West Dakota Street
(414) 321-4321

Tucked into a residential neighborhood in West Allis, the Pleasant Valley Inn isn't an easy place to find. But when you do, you'll quickly appreciate it. It is one of those charming little getaways that make you think you're in the country even though you haven't left the suburbs.

Located in the remnants of what once was Pleasant Valley Park, the building originally housed a tavern and pool hall. It was converted to a restaurant in the 1960s and redone as the Pleasant Valley Inn in the 1980s. Much of the restaurant's charm comes from its Early American decor. The restaurant has a large fireplace with an elaborate grapevine wreath hanging over it. Fresh flowers grace the tables; equally beautiful flowers are painted on the Villeroy & Boch plates.

Dinners include entrees such as grilled chicken breast medallions imperial—a grilled boneless chicken breast topped with delicate hearts of palm and plump, pink shrimp, all covered with a luscious lobster beurre blanc sauce. That rich sauce gives a distinctive, rich shellfish flavor to both the entree and the pasta served beside it. Several specials, such as grilled swordfish with a tomato, feta and pine nut sauce are offered each night. And even the bread basket is a delight. Tiny muffins and fresh puffy bread rolls are good, but the real surprise comes with Cajun rolls, which have a clump of gooey melted pimento cheese inside them.

Wednesday night is tapas night, and the list of specials includes plenty of the Spanish-inspired appetizers. If you're really lucky, paella, a rice stew with fish and meat, will be offered.

Open 5 to 9 p.m. Tuesday through Thursday; 5 to 10 p.m. Friday and Saturday; 4 to 8 p.m. Sunday. Closed Monday. Dinner $$ to $$$$. All major credit cards accepted. Smoking and nonsmoking sections available.

Price Key

$	Under $10
$$	$10 to $15
$$$	$15 to $20
$$$$	$20 to $25
$$$$$	$25 to $30

Prices are for a single entree. Menus and hours of operation frequently change. Call ahead to avoid disappointment.

▼ ▼ ▼ ▼ ▼ ▼ ▼ ▼ ▼ ▼ ▼ ▼ ▼ ▼ ▼ ▼ ▼ ▼

West Allis

Singha Thai
2237 South 108th Street
(414) 541-1234

Milwaukee has always been a city that values diversity in its restaurants. So when the first Thai restaurants opened here in the mid-1980s, they were well-received. In the years that have followed, the number of Thai restaurants has grown steadily to the point where every side of town has at least one such establishment. One of the best is Singha Thai, tucked into a strip mall on busy Highway 100 in West Allis.

In case you've never tried it, Thai food is some of the most interesting in the world, primarily because of its unusual ingredients. Some dishes use leaves from a special type of lime tree; others rely on "holy basil" (a Thai variety that has an anise flavor) and a special pungent ginger called *kha.* Add to that a love of fresh lime, chili peppers and a fish sauce (called *nam pla*) that the Thais use on everything, and you've got the basis of a rich cuisine.

Two Singha Thai appetizers are especially good. Fresh spring rolls are delicate Thai crepes filled with bean sprouts, cucumber, egg and green onion, served with sweet plum sauce. *Tod mun* are Thai fritters made with fish and green beans and served with chopped peanuts and a sweet-sour cucumber sauce. Singha Thai's version of *tom kha gai* soup is a chicken broth with coconut milk, sharpened with lemon grass (a popular ingredient in Thai food that imparts a strong citrusy taste) and full of fresh button mushrooms.

For entrees, don't miss charcoal chicken (the Thai version of barbecue), the noodle dishes (I like duck with egg noodles best) and the curries. My favorite among the latter is panang beef curry, a spicy dish with slices of meat in a hot curry sauce with basil leaves and sliced hot peppers. Several other curries are available, all in varying degrees of spiciness.

Whatever you do, save room for dessert. Thai custard and steamed tapioca pudding are both worth sampling. And for a real delight, try a Thai iced coffee or tea.

Open 11 a.m. to 9 p.m. Monday through Thursday; 11 a.m. to 10 p.m. Friday and Saturday; 4 to 9 p.m. Saturday; 4 to 9 p.m. Sunday. Lunch and dinner $ to $$$. MasterCard and Visa accepted. Smoking is allowed when the restaurant is not busy.

Index to Restaurants

52 Stafford, 43

Al Johnson's Swedish Restaurant
  and Butik, 17
Anderson's, 61
Audubon Inn, 87

Bartolotta's Lake Park Bistro, 92
Beach Club, 11
Big Mama and Uncle Fats', 14
Black Locust, 7
Blue Marlin Restaurant
  and Raw Bar, 78
Boder's on the River, 88
Bolo Country Inn, 16
Boulevard Inn, 93
Brew City BBQ, 14
Buchel's Colonial House, 110
Butterfly, 55

Café at the Pfister, 91
Café Continental, 56
Camille's, 62
Carnegie's Club Room, 50
Charcoal Inn North, 46
Charcoal Inn South, 46
Chili John's, 40
Ching Hwa, 116
Clay Market Café, 58
Clubhouse on Madeline Island, 15
Cookery, 9
Corner House, 112
Creamery, 32
Culver's, 70

De Zwann, 37
Deb & Lola's, 79
Deininger's, 108
Del-Bar Steakhouse, 75
Dick Manhardt's Inn, 61

Eagan's, 94
East Garden Chinese Restaurant, 113
Elias Inn, 61
Elm Grove Inn, 63
Elsa's on the Park, 91

English Room, 95
Erv's Mug, 61
Eve's Supper Club, 25, 28

Famous Dave's BBQ Shack, 12, 25
Fanny Hill, 5, 25
FireHouse on the River, 25
Fred's Wagon Wheel, 59
Fyfe's Corner Bistro, 80

Globe Café and Bakery, 41
Grenadier's, 96
Guide's Inn, 4

Harbor View Café, 42
Harold's, 97
Heaven City, 106
Heidel House's Grey Rock
  Mansion Restaurant, 25, 35
Hobnob, 25, 72
Hoffbrau Supper Club, 44
Hot Fish Shop, 47

Immigrant in the American Club, 36
Inn at Cedar Crossing, 20
Inn at Kristofer's, 18, 25
Izumi's, 98

Jacobi's of Hazelhurst, 13
Jerry's Old Town Inn, 14, 67
John Ernst Restaurant, 99
Judy's Kitchen, 54

Kabul Restaurant, 81
Karl Ratzsch's Old World
  Restaurant, 100
Kopp's, 71
Kroll's East, 40
Kroll's West, 40

La Bonne Femme, 33
Lake Park Bistro, 25
Leon's, 70-71
L'Etoile, 82
Library, 22
Little Red Inn, 69

121

Index to Restaurants

▼ ▼ ▼ ▼ ▼ ▼ ▼ ▼ ▼ ▼ ▼ ▼ ▼ ▼ ▼ ▼ ▼ ▼

Louise's Trattoria, 91, 101
Louisianne's, 90

M.J. Stevens, 61
Mangia Trattoria, 73
Mike and Anna's, 103
Mike's Smoke House, 14
Mimma's Café, 91
Miss Katie's Diner, 77

New Glarus Hotel, 108
Nite Cap Inn, 61
North Shore Bistro, 65

Old Rittenhouse Inn, 3
Omega Frozen Custard, 70
Oscar's Frozen Custard, 71
Osteria del Mondo, 91, 104

Pasta Per Tutti, 83
Peggy's, 29
Peking, 24
Piggy's of La Crosse, 14, 38
Plantation, 2
Pleasant Valley Inn, 119
Polaris, 25
Port Hotel, 111

Quivey's Grove, 64

Ray Radigan's, 74
Real Chili, 102
Red Circle Inn, 107
Red Geranium, 76
Restaurant, 48
Ristorante Bartolotta, 118
River Lane Inn, 57
Riversite, 89

Sally's Meat N Place, 114
Sammy's Pizza, 40
Sanford, 105
Schultz's, 46
Selensky's Grand Champion Grille, 68
Serb Memorial Hall, 60
Shack, 23

Silver Coach, 49
Singha Thai, 120
Smoky's Club, 84
Steven Wade's Café, 109

Terry's Diner, 46
Tornado Club Steak House, 85
Traditions, 39
Trattoria Stefano, 45
Trio, 6

Union Hotel, 30, 40
Union House, 66

Vintage, 51

Weisgerber Gasthaus Restaurant, 117
Wellington, 34
White Gull Inn, 10
White Stag Inn, 21
Whitetail Inn, 19
Wild Onion, 31, 40
Wilson Street Grill, 86
WolfenDale's, 115

▼ ▼ ▼ ▼ ▼ ▼ ▼ ▼ ▼ ▼ ▼ ▼ ▼ ▼ ▼ ▼ ▼

More Books on Wisconsin
From Wisconsin Trails

The Wisconsin Traveler's Companion
A Guide to Country Sights
by Jerry Apps and Julie Sutter-Blair

The W-Files
True Reports of Wisconsin's Unexplained Phenomena
by Jay Rath

Great Wisconsin Walks
by Wm. Chad McGrath

Great Weekend Adventures
from the Editors of Wisconsin Trails

Great Golf in Wisconsin
by John Hughes and Jeff Mayers

County Parks of Wisconsin
by Jeannette and Chet Bell

Best Wisconsin Bike Trips
by Phil Van Valkenberg

Best Canoe Trails of Southern Wisconsin
by Michael E. Duncanson

Wisconsin, The Story of the Badger State
by Norman K. Risjord

Barns of Wisconsin
by Jerry Apps

Mills of Wisconsin
by Jerry Apps and Allen Strang

Wisconsin Trails
P.O. Box 5650
Madison, WI 53705
(800) 236-8088